HEADWAY

STUDENT'S BOOK **PRE–INTERMEDIATE**

John & Liz Soars

Oxford University Press

LANGUAGE INPUT

SKILLS DEVELOPMENT

● READING	● SPEAKING	● LISTENING	● WRITING
Topic	Activity	Topic	Activity
'Hello, people of the world!' – People, the great communicators p.9	Discussion – People and animals p.9 Discussion – Living in capital cities, and relationships between parents and children p.11	Leaving home – A father and his daughter talk p.11 (jigsaw)	The writing input is in the Workbook. The page numbers in this column refer to the Workbook (WB). Writing letters (1) Informal letters WB p.9
How others see the British p.16 (jigsaw)	Discussion – Tourists in your country p.16 Discussion – Strict schools p.18	Life in a Japanese school p.17	Linking words (1) WB p.13 Describing a person
An extract from a James Bond story, *The Man with the Golden Gun* p.22	Retelling a story from pictures p.23	An interview with the biographer of Ian Fleming p.24	Writing a story (1) WB p.19
A magazine article about the famous store, Marks & Spencer p.29	Talking about a favourite store p.30 Group work – Devising an advertisement p.31	Five radio advertisements p.31	Filling in forms WB p.25
A questionnaire – How ambitious are you? p.36 'The right person for you' – An article from the *Today* newspaper about computer dating p.38 (jigsaw)	A class survey – How ambitious are you? p.36 Discussion – Arranged marriages p.39	How different learners of English organize their vocabulary learning p.37	Writing postcards WB p.31
'The richest man in the world' – A newspaper article about the Sultan of Brunei p.44	Describing people and places p.41 Discussion – Who are the rich people in your country? p.45	Kate Leigh talks about living in Madrid p.46	Relative clauses (1) WB p.34 Describing a place
'Paul Newman – actor, director, racing driver' – A magazine article p.52	Roleplay – Interviewing a group of musicians p.55	An interview with Paul Carrack, a pop musician p.54	Relative clauses (2) WB p.41 Writing a biography
Two special teenagers – David, a computer programmer, and Kimora, a top model p.60	Discussion – Teenagers and their parents p.62 Discussion – Giving advice about visiting your country p.64	Three people giving advice about visiting their country p.63	Writing letters (2) WB p.45 Formal letters

LANGUAGE INPUT

SKILLS DEVELOPMENT

● READING   ● SPEAKING   ● LISTENING   ● WRITING

INTRODUCTION

To the student

Welcome to Headway Pre-Intermediate!

There are three parts to learning a language in the classroom.

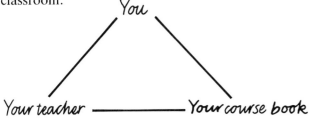

Remember! Your teacher can't learn English for you, but he/she can help. *Headway Pre-Intermediate* can't learn English for you, but it can help. What *you* do is very important if you want to learn English.

The Student's Book

You must always know *what* you are doing in class, and *why*.
Make sure you understand what this book is trying to do.
This is the organization of each unit of *Headway Pre-Intermediate*:

Presentation
You learn new grammar, and revise grammar you already know a little.

Practice
You use the grammar and you get to know it. Sometimes you speak, and sometimes you listen. Sometimes you work in pairs, and sometimes in groups.

Language review
This gives the grammar rules.

Skills development
You use English in a *real* way. You read things from newspapers, books, and magazines. You listen to English people, and English speakers from different parts of the world. And you speak a lot! Also in this part, there are some vocabulary activities to help you learn new words.

Everyday English
You learn some phrases that you need every day, and you practise English in common situations.

Grammar section
This gives you more information about the grammar. You can study it at home.

Vocabulary
At the back of the book there are vocabulary lists for each unit. You can write the translation in your language as you learn the words.

Appendices
At the back of the book there are lists of irregular verbs, dependent prepositions, and verb patterns.

Tapescripts
Your teacher has the scripts of the listening materials. Ask for a copy if you want to study them at home.

The Workbook

There are exercises to practise grammar and vocabulary, and activities to help you write in English.

Stop and Check
After every three units, there is a self-check review section. This will help you to revise what you have studied, and decide what you need to practise more.

You

In class, try to be busy all of the time. Ask questions if you want to. Don't worry about making mistakes – you can learn from your mistakes!
You need a bilingual dictionary (English – your language). Why not buy one that you can put in your pocket? You can buy a bigger dictionary later.
At the end of every lesson, you can ask your teacher two questions:

We hope you enjoy learning English!

UNIT 1

People

PRESENTATION

1 **T.1a** Read and listen to the text about Rob, a student in England.

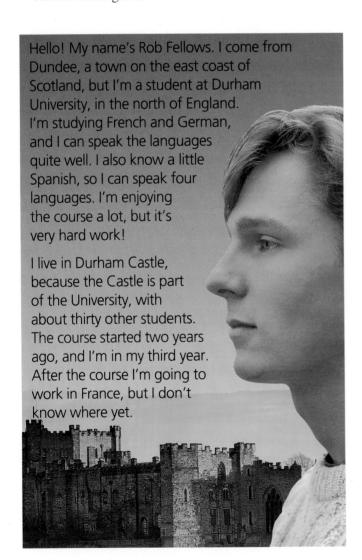

Hello! My name's Rob Fellows. I come from Dundee, a town on the east coast of Scotland, but I'm a student at Durham University, in the north of England. I'm studying French and German, and I can speak the languages quite well. I also know a little Spanish, so I can speak four languages. I'm enjoying the course a lot, but it's very hard work!

I live in Durham Castle, because the Castle is part of the University, with about thirty other students. The course started two years ago, and I'm in my third year. After the course I'm going to work in France, but I don't know where yet.

2 This is Maggie. She is also a student in England. Ask questions about her to get similar information. Use **she** and **her**.

Example
*What's **her** surname?*

a. _____ come from?
b. What _____ studying?
c. How many _____ speak?
d. Is _____ enjoying _____ ?
e. _____ live?
f. _____ live with?
g. _____ course start?
h. What _____ after the course?

3 **T.1b** Listen to Maggie, and write the answers to the questions you wrote.
Listen again to check your answers.

4 Complete the following questions to Maggie. Use **you** and **your**.
a. 'Which _____ to?'
   'I don't go to a university. I study at home.'
b. '_____ a job?'
   'Yes, a part-time job.'
c. '_____ to England?'
   'Fifteen years ago.'
d. '_____ name?'
   'Dave.'
e. '_____?'
   'He's a taxi-driver.'

7

5 Match the questions and the answers.

> 1 Where were you born?
> 2 Are you married?
> 3 What do you do?
> 4 How many children do you have?
> 5 How far is it from Dundee to Durham?
> 6 How do you come to school?
> 7 Why are you learning English?

> a. By bus.
> b. I'm a teacher.
> c. Three.
> d. In Australia.
> e. Because I need it for my job.
> f. About 120 miles.
> g. No, I'm single.

● Grammar questions

She **comes** from Australia.
She's **studying** art.

– What tenses are the two verb forms in these sentences?
– What is the difference between them?

PRACTICE

1 Speaking and listening

1 Work in pairs.
Ask and answer questions about each other.

> Where do you live?
> What do you do?
> Why are you learning English?

2 Think of some questions to ask your teacher.

> Are you married?
> What do you like doing at the weekend?
> What sort of music do you like?

2 Grammar

Decide which is the correct verb form.
a. Maria *comes/is coming* from Spain.
b. She *speaks/is speaking* French, Spanish, and English.
c. Today *she wears/is wearing* jeans and a T-shirt.
d. She *smokes/is smoking* twenty cigarettes a day.
e. She *doesn't smoke/isn't smoking* now. She's in class.

3 Speaking and listening

Work in small groups.
Ask and answer the following questions.
a. Do you smoke?
   If you do, how many cigarettes do you smoke a day?
   Are you smoking now?
b. Does your teacher smoke?
   Is he/she smoking now?
c. Do you wear glasses?
   Are you wearing glasses now?
d. What are you wearing?
   What is your teacher wearing?
e. Look at the other students.
   Who is laughing?   Who is listening?
   Who is speaking?   Who is writing?

● Language review

Question forms

1 Look at the following question words.
   What do you do? – I'm a student.
   Who is your teacher? – David is.
   Where is Melbourne? – In Australia.
   When do lessons start? – At 9.00.
   Why are you learning English? – Because I need it for my job.
   How do you come to school? – By bus.
   Whose is this pen? – It's Peter's.

2 **What** and **which** can be followed by a noun. **How** can be followed by an adjective or an adverb.
   What time is it?
   What kind of car do you have?
   Which pen do you want, the blue one or the red one?
   How old is she?
   How often do you play tennis?

Present Continuous

The Present Continuous is used to express an activity happening now or around now.

Translate

I'm learning English because I need it for my job.

He smokes twenty cigarettes a day.

He's smoking a cigarette now.

▶ **Grammar reference: page 120.**

SKILLS DEVELOPMENT

● Reading and speaking

Pre-reading task
Work in pairs.
1 Write down the names of as many animals as you can. What can they do that people can't?

Example
Birds can fly.

2 What can people do that animals can't?

Example
We can write poetry.

3 Look up the following words in your bilingual dictionary and write down the translation.

jungle (*n*)	**to record** (*v*) e.g.
species (*n*)	information in a book
numerous (*adj*)	**sense** (*n*)
powerful (*adj*)	**to choose** (*v*)
joke (*n*)	**to look after** (*v*)
	to destroy (*v*)

Reading
Now read the article.

1 Here are four questions which introduce the four paragraphs in the article. They are not in the right order. Write down the correct question for each paragraph.
   a. How are people and animals different?
   b. How many people are there?
   c. What can people choose to do?
   d. What is the biggest difference between people and animals?
2 Check *your* lists of what people and animals can and can't do. What ideas did you have that are not in the article?
3 How do people communicate?
4 Why is writing a special kind of communication?

What do you think?
1 Do animals have a sense of past and future?
2 How do animals communicate?
3 In what ways are we looking after the world, and in what ways are we destroying it?

Hello, people of the World!

こんにちは   Salut!   你好   — Ciao   صباح الخير   ¡Hola!

[?]

There are five billion people in the world and they live in all different corners of it. They live on the snow and ice of the Poles and in the tropical jungles on the equator. They have climbed the
5 highest mountains and walked on the sea bed. Some of them have even left the earth and visited the moon.

[?]

The human species is the most numerous and the most powerful of all the animals on earth. How did
10 this happen? In many ways, animals can do things better than we can. Dogs can smell and hear better than we can. Cats can see in the dark. Birds can fly thousands of miles away and return to the same place every year. But we *are* different.
15 No other animal builds cathedrals, plays football,

tells jokes, gets married, has prisons, writes symphonies, elects presidents, or goes to the moon.

[?]

There is one thing above all that makes people and
20 animals different. People love to talk – talk – talk. We are the great communicators! And we can communicate so many things in so many ways – with our faces, our hands, our bodies, and our voices. Most important of all, we can record what
25 we say and think in writing, so that we can communicate through time. We have a sense of past and future, not just present.

[?]

We are the only species that can change the world, and we are the only species that can choose either
30 to look after our world or to destroy it.

9

● Vocabulary

Using a bilingual dictionary

1 Look at this extract from the *Oxford French Minidictionary*. Notice how the entry is organized.

The part of speech
(*n* = noun)

The pronunciation
in phonetic symbols

Nouns and verbs are
in the same entry.

The translation

Information in brackets
(...) helps you to find
the right translation.

book /bʊk/ *n.* livre *m*: (*of tick-ets, etc.*) carnet *m*. ~s (*comm.*) comptes *m. pl, v.t.* (*reserve*) retenir; (*write down*) inscrire. ~ *v.i.* retenir des places ~**able** *a.* qu'on peut retenir. (**fully**) ~**ed.** complet. ~**ing office,** guichet *m*.

bookcase /'bʊkkeɪs/ *n.* biblioth-èque *f.*
bookseller /'bʊkselə(r)/ *n.* libraire *m./f.*
bookshop /'bʊkʃɒp/ *n.* librairie *f.*
bookstall /'bʊkstɔːl/ *n.* kiosque (à journaux) *m.*

Other words made with
book come afterwards.

~ means *Repeat the headword*, so this word is **bookable**.

2 Compare this with your own dictionary.
   Does your dictionary give as much information?
   Does it give the information in the same way?

3 Look at the following. Is the word a noun, verb, adjective, adverb, preposition, or past tense?

bread	beautiful	on	hot	in	came
went	never	eat	quickly	write	letter

Write another example of each word class.
What is the abbreviation for these word classes in your dictionary?

4 Many words have more than one meaning, and you must be careful when you use your dictionary to find the right definition.
In the following sentences, the words in *italics* have more than one meaning. Look up each word, find the right meaning, and translate it.
   a. Guido's is a popular restaurant, so you have to *book* a table in advance.
   b. I'm not a *fan* of the Rolling Stones. Their music is too loud.
   c. Wood doesn't *sink* in water. It stays on the top.
   d. Your mother is a very *kind* lady.
   e. Holland is a *flat* country.
   f. Car workers are on *strike*. They want more money.
   g. Don't forget to turn the *tap* off. Water is expensive.
   h. Do you have *change* for a five-pound note?
   i. I don't like *mean* people.
   j. Give me a *ring* tonight. I'll be home at 7.00.
   k. There's a *branch* of most banks in all big towns.
   l. There was a good *play* on television last night.
   m. My suitcase is in the car *boot*.

5 Use your dictionary to find the English word for the following everyday objects.

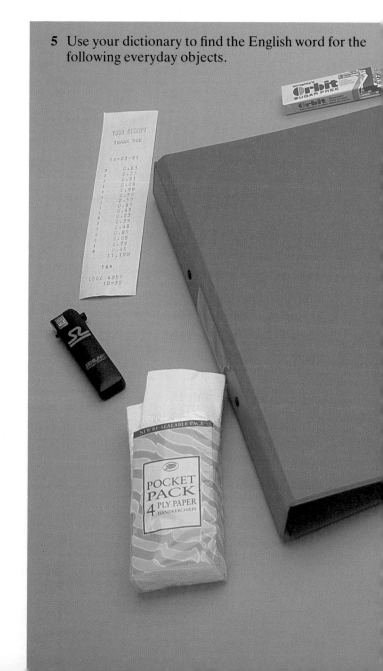

● Listening and speaking

Leaving home

Pre-listening task

Discuss the following questions in groups.

1 Do you live in the capital city of your country?
   a. If you do
      – do you like it?
      – what are its attractions?
      – is it safe?
   b. If you don't
      – would you like to?
      – have you visited your capital city?
      – what attractions does it have that your town
        doesn't have?

2 What is the population of your capital city?
   What is special about it?

3 When you go away from home (for a short or a long
   time), do you *keep in touch*? How?

Jigsaw listening

Divide into two groups.

T.2a Group **A** You will hear David Snow, who lives
in the north-west of England, talking about his only
daughter, Jackie.

T.2b Group **B** You will hear Jackie, David Snow's
daughter, talking about her life in London.

Read and answer the questions on page 12 as you listen.
(You can't answer them all!)

Look around the room you are in.
Think of five things you don't know the words
for in English. Look them up!

Comprehension check
1 Why did Jackie come to London?
2 When did she come?
3 Where is she living?
4 Who is she living with?
5 What's she doing in London?
6 What does her boyfriend do?
7 What does she do at the weekend?
8 What does she think of living in London?
9 How often does she keep in touch?
10 What does she think of her parents?

When you have answered your questions, find a partner from the other group.
Compare your answers and swap information.

What do you think?
1 Is Jackie's father right to be so worried about his daughter? Was Jackie right to leave home at eighteen?

2 Use your dictionary to find out what *generation gap* means. Is there a generation gap between you and your parents? Between you and your children?

3 In your country, at what age
   – can people get married? – can they smoke?
   – can they vote?   – can they drive?

● **Everyday English**

Social English

1 We say certain things at certain times.

Match a line in **A** with a line in **B**.

A	B
Hello, Jane!	Sleep well!
How are you?	Yes. Can I help you?
See you tomorrow!	Good morning!
Good night!	Fine, thanks.
Good morning!	Not at all. Don't mention it.
Cheers!	Thanks.
Excuse me!	Thanks! Same to you!
Bless you!	That's very kind. Thank you.
Have a good weekend!	Bye!
Thank you very much indeed.	Hi, Peter!
Make yourself at home.	Good health!

2 [**T.3**] Listen to the tape to check your answers. When do we say these things? Practise saying them!

The National Gallery

Dear Mum and Dad
Tony and I were here today. It was really interesting.
I hope you're both well.
I'll phone you next Sunday as usual.
Lots of love
Jackie

London: The National Gallery

Mr and Mrs D Snow
33 St Bede's Close
Lancaster
Lancashire

LA1 3BU

UNIT 2

Present Simple – Have/have got – Numbers

Lifestyles

PRESENTATION

A market research organization interviewed 8,000 people in different European countries to find out about their lifestyles.

1 Which country do the following flags belong to?

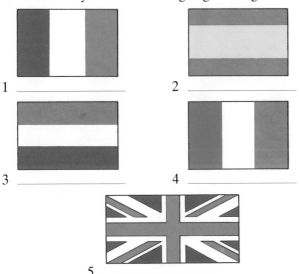

1 _____   2 _____

3 _____   4 _____

5 _____

2 Work in pairs.
Which flag goes with which text?

This country has a population of 38.8 million. It is unusual in Europe because it has more single young men than single young women. It has about 20% unemployment but the tourist industry brings high seasonal employment. The people often borrow money but rarely borrow to buy houses. Many, however, have second holiday homes. Most people cook with gas, not electricity. They like low-alcohol drinks.
a

This country has a population of 14.7 million. The people are very cosmopolitan. They travel a lot, learn foreign languages, and buy many things from other countries. The people have a high standard of living. They own the most stereos and video cameras. They don't buy many motorbikes but they buy a lot of bicycles. The country has a large student population, and the highest percentage of single people.
b

This country has a population of 55.5 million. It has a strong economy and a lot of high technology industries, but not many people have home computers. The people have small families and love food, but only their own national food. They smoke and drink more than their European neighbours, and they have more health problems.
c

This country has a population of 56.5 million. It has the most marriages, but also the most divorces in Europe. Many people use credit cards, and they often borrow money, particularly to buy houses. They don't save very much. They own the most videos and home computers in Europe. They like food from many countries, but prefer their own national food. People from other countries generally don't like their food.
d

This country has a population of 57.3 million. The people have large families and often own a second holiday home. They love cars and motorbikes and own more than all other European countries. They spend a lot of money on clothes, but they don't buy many stereos and videos. Nearly every country in Europe loves the food of this country.
e

3 Is one of these your country? If so, do you think the information is correct? If your country is not here, give some similar facts about it.

● Grammar questions

– What tense are all the verb forms in the texts? Why?
– Why is **have** and not **have got** used in the texts?
– What is the difference between them?

PRACTICE

1 Grammar

Notice that **have** and **have got** are used in different ways in the question, short answer, and negative forms.

> Do you have a car?
> Have you got a car?

> Yes, I do.
> Yes, I have.

> I don't have a computer.
> I haven't got a computer.

Work in pairs.
Ask and answer questions about the following:
– a camera
– a stereo
– a computer
– a bicycle
– a credit card

– brothers and sisters
– your parents/a holiday home
– your sister/a car
– your brother/a motorbike

2 Speaking and listening

1 You are going to ask and answer questions about the people in the charts. First prepare the questions.

Town/country	– Where does he . . . from?
Family	– . . . married?
	– Does she have . . . ?
	– Has he got . . . ?
	– How many . . . ?
Occupation	– What . . . do?
Free time/holiday	– What does she . . . in her free time?
	– Where . . . go on holiday?
Present activity	– What . . . doing at the moment?

2 Work in pairs. **Student A** Look at the chart on this page.
Student B Look at the chart on page 119.
Ask and answer questions to complete your charts.

Student A

NAME AND AGE	TOWN AND COUNTRY	FAMILY	OCCUPATION	FREE TIME / HOLIDAY	PRESENT ACTIVITY
MIGUEL 26					
CHANTAL 34					
EMMA 15	- Oxford - England	- parents divorced - one brother	- schoolgirl	- pop music - every holiday with her father in Scotland	- working hard for her exams
MARIO and RITA CUMINO 65 and 63	- Siena - Italy	- one married daughter - one grandson	- retired company director	- opera - visit their daughter in America every summer	- preparing to go to America

3 Writing and listening

Here is an interview with Emma.

1 Complete the interviewer's part.

Interviewer	Hello, Emma. Thank you for agreeing to do this interview, especially as I believe you're studying for your exams at the moment.
Emma	Yes, I am. But I'm happy to do the interview.
Interviewer	Now, the questions. First of all, ...?
Emma	Oxford, in England.
Interviewer	And ....?
Emma	At home with my mother. You see, my parents are divorced.
Interviewer	Ah! I'm sorry about that. ....?
Emma	Yes, I have. I've got a brother.
Interviewer	..................................?
Emma	No, he's younger. He's twelve.
Interviewer	And ....?
Emma	Well, he's either playing football or watching TV. That's what he always does after school.
Interviewer	And ....?
Emma	He lives in Scotland, near Edinburgh.
Interviewer	..................................?
Emma	Well, we see him quite often. We spend every school holiday with him.
Interviewer	Now a final question, Emma. ....?
Emma	I listen to music, especially pop music.
Interviewer	That's great, Emma. I've got all the information I need. Thank you very much.

2 **T.4** Now listen and compare your answers.

3 Write a similar dialogue between the interviewer and another person in the chart.

● Language review

Present Simple

The Present Simple is used to express a present habit, or an action which happens again and again. It is also used to express a fact which is always true, or true for a long time.

> **Translate**
>
> She often goes to the cinema.
>
> _____
>
> He comes from Majorca.
>
> _____

Present Continuous

Read the Language review about the Present Continuous on page 8 again.

> **Translate**
>
> He speaks five languages.
>
> _____
>
> He's speaking French at the moment.
>
> _____

Have/have got

Have and **have got** mean the same, but **have** plus the **do** forms are more formal, so you see them more in written English.

> *Does America **have** a large population?*
> *Yes. It **has** a population of 247 million.*

▶ **Grammar reference: page 121.**

SKILLS DEVELOPMENT

● Reading and speaking

How others see the British

You are going to read a magazine article about three people who came from other countries to live in Britain.

Pre-reading task

1 Work alone. Close your eyes and think of Britain. Write down the first five things you thought of.

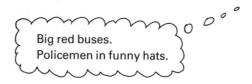

Big red buses.
Policemen in funny hats.

2 Work in groups.
Compare your lists.
Why did you think of those things?

Reading
Work in three groups.
Group A You are going to read about Kimiko, from Japan.
Group B You are going to read about Xavier, from France.
Group C You are going to read about Margaretha, from Norway.

15

Read your extract. Use your dictionary if you want.
Answer the following questions.
1 Why did he/she come to Britain?
2 What does he/she do?
3 Find one thing he/she likes about Britain, and one thing he/she doesn't like so much.

Kimiko – Japan

There are now more than two dozen Japanese companies in Tyne and Wear in the northeast of England. Many Japanese
5 families now live there.

Kimiko Kinoshita Wood came to Britain as a bride six years ago. 'There is much more freedom for women here,' she
10 says. 'It is sometimes difficult for Japanese women to adjust.'
For Kimiko, the change was easy because she is a translator and speaks English fluently. Also, she has an English husband. 'Attitudes to women are very different,' she says.
15 'Japanese wives come to Britain and after a while they discover they can have a life of their own outside the home. They don't have that kind of freedom in Japan.'
In Japan it is unusual to see men shopping with their wives, helping in the house, or babysitting. But Kimiko's husband,
20 John, a shipping engineer, happily lends a hand with the children. John says that Japanese husbands soon adapt in Britain, and seem to relax more with their families.
Education is one thing that worries Kimiko. In Japan, children go to school six days a week and work much harder
25 than English children. Another complaint is that shops don't have many clothes for small women!

Xavier – France

When Xavier Dupont came to Britain, his friends in Paris said he'd hate it. However, Xavier, a 26-year-old chef,
30 says they were wrong.
'French people imagine that Britain is a cold, miserable country where everyone dresses badly, you can't see anything for fog, and the food is the
35 worst on the planet. I don't agree.'
Xavier insists that the British look good because they don't follow fashion so seriously. He enjoys shopping in Britain because there are so many fresh things in the supermarkets. He particularly likes the street
40 markets.
However he has some complaints. He thinks that British men don't show enough consideration or appreciation of the women. Also, he doesn't like British bathrooms where you stand or sit in the bath to have a shower! Last of all, he feels
45 that shops and restaurants close far too often and far too early.

Margaretha – Norway

In Britain, Margaretha Simons can be a full-time housewife, at home with her
50 four children. This, she says, is unusual in her native Norway because almost all Norwegian women go out to work,
55 partly because there are more crèches. It is also unusual in Norway to have more than two children.
Margaretha, who is 43, met her British husband,
60 Noel, a university professor, while she was learning English in Cambridge.
'I find British people friendly,' she says. 'New neighbours invite you for coffee, introduce their children, and take you to the shops. The men are more courteous
65 and romantic than Norwegian men.'
However she doesn't like everything. She thinks British houses are not built well – even modern houses have a lot of draughts. Also, there is too much litter on the streets and by the sides of the motorways. She
70 likes fresh British food, but at first she did not like the tea because it looked cloudy and grey. Now she is addicted to it, and has cups of tea all the time!

Comprehension check
1 Find a partner from each of the other two groups. Compare and swap information.
2 Read the other two extracts. Help each other with any new words.
3 Look at the following statements about the three people. Which are true? Which are false?
   a. Japanese men find it difficult to relax in Britain because their wives are so busy all the time.
   b. Xavier thinks the British dress well.
   c. Kimiko and Margaretha both have English husbands.
   d. Both Xavier and Margaretha have a good opinion of British men.
   e. Kimiko met her husband in Japan but Margaretha met hers in England.
   f. They all enjoy shopping in Britain. They have no complaints about British shops.
   g. Both Xavier and Margaretha have complaints about the design of British houses.
   h. Generally they all seem happy to live in Britain.

What do you think?
1 What do tourists like doing in your country? Where do they go? What do they do?
2 Do you know any foreigners living in your country? What do they like about it? What do they find different?

Vocabulary

Vocabulary networks

It is useful to record words which are associated in
networks because it can help you to remember them.
You can do this in a list or in the form of a diagram like
the one below.
The following are all electrical household goods. Use
your dictionaries to check the meaning and (if possible)
the pronunciation of any you do not know, then fill in
the spaces. Some are already filled to help you.

air-conditioning	cooker	dishwasher
microwave oven	spotlight	fan freezer
fridge food mixer	home computer	iron
kettle lamp hi-fi system		vacuum cleaner
Walkman video	washing machine	
word processor	CD player	fan heater

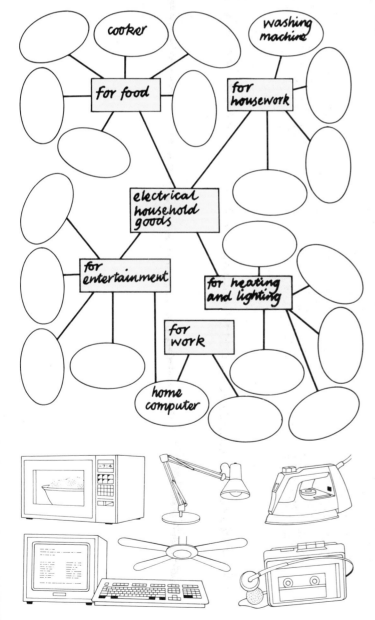

Discussion

1 Which rooms do you usually find these things in?
2 Which do you think are very important/not so
   important to everyday home life? Why?
3 Which do you have in your own home?

Now choose a room in your house and make a similar
diagram of some of the things in it.
Use your dictionary to look up any words you want to
know. When your diagram is complete use it to help you
describe the room to a partner.

Listening

Life in a Japanese school

You are going to listen to a radio interview with
Graham Grant, an English teacher who recently spent
two years teaching in Japan.

Pre-listening task

The following words and phrases are in the interview.
Check the meaning and the pronunciation in your
dictionary.

attitude (*n*)	strict (*adj*)
retire (*v*)	bow (*v*) /baʊ/ e.g. to bow
competitive (*adj*)	to the Queen
discipline (*n*)	politeness (*n*)
row (*n*) /rəʊ/ e.g. to sit in	respect (*n*)
the front row	rude (*adj*)

Listening for information

T.5 Listen to the interview and answer the
questions.
1 Why is education so important in Japan?
2 'Children must do well at school.' Why?
3 At what age do they start to work hard?
4 What do they do in class?
5 What do they do in the evening?
6 Do they have a long holiday?
7 How do they spend their weekends and holidays?

Asking and answering questions

Divide into two groups. Each group has four answers to questions about the interview. Write the questions, then ask the other group to answer them.

Group A

1 _____?

He's teaching Japanese in England.

2 _____?

They usually stay from the time they leave school or university until they retire.

3 _____?

About forty.

4 _____?

Because it is rude to question a teacher.

Group B

1 _____?

Six.

2 _____?

Three or four hours every night.

3 _____?

Yes, they do, because they are never bored.

4 _____?

She is probably watching TV.

What do you think?

1 Are Japanese schools like schools in your country?
2 What are the advantages and disadvantages of strict schools?

● Everyday English

Numbers

1 Notice that we say **and** after the hundreds.

783	*seven hundred **and** eighty-three*
408	*four hundred **and** eight*
334,000	*three hundred **and** thirty-four thousand*

Practise saying the following numbers.

277	489	612	5,870	3,923
15,804	118,307	165,000,000		

2 It is easy to confuse **13/30**, **14/40**, etc. when you hear them.

The stress patterns are usually like this:

●• thirty forty fifty sixty seventy eighty ninety

●• thirteen fourteen fifteen sixteen seventeen eighteen nineteen

When we count, the patterns are as above, but they can change with the 'teen' numbers. When the teen numbers are followed by a noun, the pattern is still ●•, but when the number is on its own, the pattern is •●.

She's fifteen (●•) years old.
She's fifteen (•●).

T.6a Underline the number you hear.

a 16/60   **b** 15/50   **c** 18/80   **d** 90/19   **e** 30/13

Prices

Look at the way we write and say the following prices.

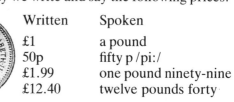

Written	Spoken
£1	a pound
50p	fifty p /piː/
£1.99	one pound ninety-nine
£12.40	twelve pounds forty

1 **T.6b** You will hear twelve short recordings. In each one there is a number. Write down the number you hear.

2 What's the exchange rate between sterling and your currency?

Example
There are about ten French francs to the pound.

How much do you pay for a three-course meal in your country? What about hamburger and chips? How much is a hotel room? How much is a packet of cigarettes?

3 Write down ten numbers and prices.
Dictate them to a partner.

UNIT 3

Past Simple – Past Continuous – Time expressions

Fact and fiction

PRESENTATION

1 Here are the past tense forms of twelve irregular verbs. Write in the base forms.

spend	spent	_____	caught
_____	sank	_____	ate
_____	left	_____	broke
_____	met	_____	saw
_____	heard	_____	could
_____	had	_____	took

2 Read the text. Use your dictionary to help.

REAL LIFE DRAMA

COUPLE WHO SURVIVED AN AMAZING 66 DAYS AT SEA

A couple from Miami, Bill and Simone Butler, spent sixty-six days in a life-raft in the seas of Central America after their yacht sank. They survived
5 in very good condition.

Twenty-one days after they left Panama in their yacht, *Siboney*, they met some whales. 'They started to hit the side of the boat,' said Bill, 'and

10 then suddenly we heard water.' Two minutes later, the yacht was sinking. They jumped into the life-raft and watched the boat go under the water.

For twenty days they had tins of
15 food, biscuits, and bottles of water. They also had a fishing-line and a machine to make salt water into

3 **T.7** You will hear a radio report of the same story, but the reporter sometimes has the wrong information! Listen and correct her.

Examples
They weren't from New York! They were from Miami!
They didn't spend sixty days at sea! They spent sixty-six days at sea!

drinking water – two things which saved their lives. They caught eight
20 to ten fish a day and ate them raw. Then the line broke. 'So we had no more fish until something very

strange happened. Some sharks came to feed, and the fish under the
25 raft were afraid and came to the surface. I caught them with my hands.'

About twenty ships passed them, but no one saw them. After fifty
30 days at sea their life-raft was beginning to break up. Then suddenly it was all over. A fishing boat saw them and picked them up. They couldn't stand up, so the captain
35 carried them onto his boat and took them to Costa Rica. Their two months at sea was over.

19

4 Work in pairs.
Ask and answer questions about the drama.

> How many days were they at sea?

> Sixty-six.

> Where did it happen?

> In the seas of Central America.

> Did they have a fishing boat?

> No, they had a yacht.

● Grammar questions

– What tense are nearly all the verbs in the article? Why?
– How do we form the question?
– How do we form the negative?

PRACTICE

1 Grammar

Write in the Past Simple of the following verbs.

start	_____	pass	_____
jump	_____	pick	_____
watch	_____	survive	_____
happen	_____	save	_____

How is the regular past tense formed?
How is the past tense formed when the verb ends in '**e**'?

carry	_____	marry	_____
study	_____		

How is the past tense formed when the verb ends in a consonant + **y**?

be	_____	go	_____
buy	_____	hit	_____
come	_____	know	_____
do	_____	make	_____
fall	_____	ring	_____
feel	_____	say	_____
find	_____	send	_____
fly	_____	swim	_____
give	_____	throw	_____

You must learn irregular verbs! There is a list on page 141.

2 Speaking and listening

Work in pairs.
Ask and answer questions.

> What did you do
> – last night?
> – last weekend?
> – on your last birthday?
> – on your last holiday?

> I watched TV / went swimming ...

● Language review

Past Simple

The Past Simple expresses a past action that is now finished.

Translate
I saw Peter yesterday.
What time did you see him?
I didn't speak to him.

▶ Grammar reference: page 122.

PRESENTATION

1 Here are the headlines from three newspaper articles. Use your dictionary to check any words you don't know.

MIRACLE ESCAPE

CHANNEL CHAMPION

PILOTLESS JET CRASHES

2 Read the articles quickly.
Which headline goes with which article?

Put the verbs below each article into the correct gap. Put them into the Past Simple.

Four-year-old Mark Harris from Bristol _____ 60 feet from a bridge into the River Avon. The river carried him towards a waterfall and _____ him onto some rocks. Fortunately, three older boys _____ Mark. They quickly pulled him out and _____ the police.

> fall   ring   see   throw

An American jet pilot _____ from Fort Worth, but the jet's engines _____ wrong. The pilot ejected, but the plane didn't crash. The engines _____ working again. The jet _____ for more than one hour over three states. Finally it crashed near Lincoln, Nebraska. It _____ some trees in a field. Fortunately no one was hurt.

> begin   fly   hit   take off   go

Twelve-year-old Thomas Gregory from London is the youngest person to swim the English Channel. He _____ the 31 miles in just 11 hours 55 minutes. He _____ hot tomato soup because he _____ so cold in the water. Often he _____ not see anything and that was the worst thing. He was very pleased when he finally arrived on the beach in France.

> can   drink   feel   swim

3 The phrases below go in the articles. Which article do they go in? Where exactly do they go in the article?

Example

Four-year-old Mark Harris from Bristol _____ 60 feet from a bridge into the River Avon. The river carried him towards a waterfall and _____ him onto some rocks. Fortunately, three older boys _____ Mark. They quickly pulled him out and _____ the police.

(*who were fishing*)

- when he was running after his dog
- while he was swimming
- where his parents were waiting for him
- where a farmer was working
- because the sun was shining in his eyes
- while it was flying over New Mexico

● Grammar question

- What tense are the verbs in question **3**? Why?

PRACTICE

1 Grammar

1 Work in pairs.
  Decide which is the correct verb form.
  a. I *saw/was seeing* a very good programme on TV last night.
  b. While I *shopped/was shopping* this morning, I *lost/was losing* my money. I don't know how.
  c. Last week the police *stopped/were stopping* Alan in his car because he *travelled/was travelling* at over eighty miles an hour.
  d. 'How *did you cut/were you cutting* your finger?'
  e. 'I *cooked/was cooking* and I dropped the knife.'

2 Put the verb in brackets in the correct verb form, Past Simple or Past Continuous.
  a. While I _____ (come) to work this morning, I _____ (meet) an old friend.
  b. I _____ (not want) to get up this morning. It _____ (rain) and it was cold, and my bed was so warm.
  c. I _____ (listen) to the news on the radio when the phone _____ (ring).
  d. But when I _____ (pick) up the phone, there was no one there.
  e. I said 'Hello' to the children, but they didn't say anything because they _____ (watch) television.

2 Speaking and listening

Work in pairs.
Ask and answer questions.

> Where were you, and what were you doing
> - at three o'clock this morning?
> - at eight o'clock this morning?
> - two years ago?
> - in August last year?
> - this time yesterday?

> I was in bed / reading ...

3 Writing

Work in groups of four.
Think of a recent news story – something that happened in your town, your country, or the world. Write down the story, and give some wrong information. When you have finished, read out your story. The rest of the class will correct you!

● Language review

Past Continuous

The Past Continuous is used to express an activity in progress around a point of time in the past. The activity began before the action expressed by the Past Simple.

> **Translate**
>
> When we arrived, she was making supper.
>
> When we arrived, she made supper.

▶ Grammar reference: page 122.

SKILLS DEVELOPMENT

● Reading and speaking

Pre-reading task

1 Here are the titles of some books. They all have the same hero. Do you know who he is? Do you know the name of the author of the books?

2 These books were all made into films which are famous in many countries. Do you know the translation of any of the titles in your language?

3 You are going to read an extract from *The Man with the Golden Gun*. The pictures illustrate the story but they are not in the right order.
Look at the pictures and try to work out the story.

Reading

Now read the text and number the pictures to fit the story.

When James Bond got back to his hotel room it was midnight. His windows were closed and the air-conditioning was on. Bond switched it off and opened the windows. His heart was still thumping in
5 his chest. He breathed in the air with relief, then had a shower and went to bed.

At 3.30 he was dreaming, not very peacefully, of the three black-coated men with red eyes and angry white teeth, when suddenly he woke up. He
10 listened. There was a noise. It was coming from the window. Someone was moving behind the curtains. James Bond took his gun from under his pillow, got quietly out of bed, and crept slowly along the wall towards the window. Someone was breathing
15 behind the curtains. Bond pulled them back with one quick movement. Golden hair shone silver in the moonlight.

'Mary Goodnight!' Bond cursed. 'What the hell are you doing here?'
20 'Quick, James! Help me in!' she whispered urgently.

Bond put down his gun and tried to pull her through the open window. At the last moment her foot caught in the curtain and the window banged
25 shut with a noise like a gunshot. Bond cursed again.

Mary Goodnight whispered, 'I'm terribly sorry, James!'

'Sh! Sh!' said Bond, and quickly led her across the
30 room to the bathroom. He turned on the light and
the shower. They sat down on the side of the bath.
     Bond asked again. 'What the hell are you doing
here? What's the matter?'
     'James, I was so worried. A "Most Immediate"
35 message came from HQ this evening. A top KGB
man, using the name Hendriks, is staying at this
hotel. I knew you were looking for him, but he knows
you're here. He's looking for you!'
     'I know,' said Bond. 'That man's here all right. So
40 is a gunman called Scaramanga. Mary, did HQ say
if Hendriks has got a description of me?'
     'No, he hasn't. You were just described as secret
agent James Bond.'
     'Thanks, Mary. Now I must get you out of here.
45 Don't worry about me, just tell HQ that you gave me
the message, OK?'
     'OK, James.' She stood up and looked into his
eyes: 'Please take care, James.'
     'Sure, sure.' Bond turned off the shower and
50 opened the bathroom door. 'Now, come on.'
     A voice came from the darkness of the bedroom:
     'This is not your lucky day, Mr Bond. Come here
both of you. Put your hands behind your necks!'
     Scaramanga walked to the door and turned on the
55 lights. His golden gun was pointing directly at James
Bond.

Comprehension check

Use your dictionary to check vocabulary where
necessary.

Are the following statements about the text true or
false? Say why.
1 James Bond felt frightened and worried when he got
   back to his hotel room.
2 A man with a gun woke Bond at 3.30 a.m.
3 Bond was very pleased to see Mary Goodnight.
4 Bond's gun went off while he was pulling Mary
   through the window.
5 Mary and James talked in the bathroom because they
   thought it was safer there than in the bedroom.
6 Hendriks knew that Bond was in the hotel.
7 Bond didn't know that Hendriks was looking for him.
8 Mary Goodnight likes James a lot.
9 James helped Mary get out of the hotel.

Vocabulary and grammar work

1 The following verbs appear in the text in their Past
  Simple form. Find them in the text and write them
  next to the base form.

have	*had*	breathe		wake
take		creep		shine
whisper		put		try
catch		lead		sit
know		give		stand

  Which ones are irregular?

2 Make a list of all the parts of the body you can find in
  the text.

Speaking

Use the pictures to retell the story in your own words.
Begin like this:
When James Bond got back to his hotel, he . . .

23

● Vocabulary

Verbs and nouns that go together

1 Good dictionaries (bilingual and monolingual) show you which words often go together.
Here are two extracts from the *Oxford Elementary Learner's Dictionary of English*.

> **joke** /dʒəʊk/ *n* something that you say to make people laugh: *He told us a very funny joke.*

One verb that often goes with the noun **joke** is **tell**.

> **draw²** *v* (*past part.* drawn /drɔːn/, *past tense* drew /druː/) **1** make pictures with a pen, pencil, etc.: *Degas drew wonderful pictures of horses.*

One noun that often goes with the verb **draw** is **picture**.

2 Match a line in **A** with a line in **B**. Use your dictionary if necessary.

A	B
wear	the washing-up
tell	a lie
drive	a photograph
take	a cheque
do	a van
make	a suit
cash	a phone call

A	B
post	a suitcase
ride	a taxi
pack	a meal
pay	a letter
order	a film on TV
watch	a horse
take	a bill

3 Ask and answer questions beginning *When did you last...?* with the words in the exercise above.

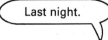
When did you last do the washing-up?   Last night.

Words and prepositions that go together

A dictionary shows you which preposition goes with a word.

> **listen** /ˈlɪsn/ *v* **listen to** hear sounds carefully; try to hear sounds: *Did you listen to the news on the radio this morning?*

Put a preposition into each gap.
a. I'm waiting _____ the postman to arrive.
b. Look _____ that picture! Isn't it beautiful!
c. I'm looking _____ Mary. Is she here?
d. She works _____ BP, a big petrol company.
e. If you have a problem, ask _____ help.
f. Are you interested _____ modern art?

g. Did you know that Alan is married _____ Barbara?
h. Can I speak _____ you for a minute?
i. Your shirt is similar _____ mine. Where did you buy it?
j. I agree _____ you about most things, but not politics.
k. My daugher is afraid _____ dogs.
l. Are you good _____ tennis?

There is a list of words + preposition on page 142.

● Listening and writing

An interview with a biographer

Pre-listening task
You are going to hear a radio interview with Lucy Parker. She wrote a biography of Ian Fleming, the author of the James Bond books.
Ian Fleming had a number of jobs before he became a writer. Which of the following jobs do you think he had? Use your dictionary to check any you don't know.

banker	soldier	stockbroker
journalist	translator	spy
Member of Parliament	member of MI5	member of Naval Intelligence

Listening

T.8   Listen and answer the following questions.

1 Which jobs *did* Ian Fleming have before he became a writer?

2 The interviewer says at the beginning of the interview:
I think the thing that many people want to know is: 'How much is Ian Fleming, the author, like the hero of his books, James Bond?'
While you listen, make quick notes of ways in which you think he was like James Bond.

Comprehension check

1 When was Ian Fleming born?
2 How was he different from his brothers?
3 Where did he go in 1930?
4 Why didn't he join the Foreign Office?
5 Was he working as a journalist when the Second World War started?
6 Which countries did he visit during the war?
7 What kind of lifestyle did he have?
8 Was he a healthy man?
9 What three important things happened in Jamaica in 1952?
10 When did he die? How old was he?
11 The following numbers are in the interview. What do they refer to?

    nine   sixty   fourteen   forty million

Writing

Write a short biography either of yourself or of an author you know and like.

Include: Date and place of birth
               Some family background
               Education
               Some important events

● Everyday English

Time expressions

1 Notice how we can say a date in two ways:

8/1/74   the eighth of January, nineteen seventy-four
            January the eighth, nineteen seventy-four

In pairs, practise saying the following dates.

4 June   25 August 31 July   1 March   3 February
21/1/1988 2/12/1976 5/4/1980 11/6/1965 18/10/1989

  T.9   Listen to the pronunciation of the dates, and practise them.

2 When is your birthday? What is your date of birth? What days are national holidays in your country?

3 Look at the chart.

at	in	no preposition
at six o'clock	in the morning / afternoon / evening	today
at midnight		yesterday
at Christmas	in December	tomorrow
at the weekend	in summer	the day after tomorrow
	in 1985	the day before yesterday
on	in two weeks' time	last night
on Saturday		last week
on Monday morning		next month
on Christmas Day		yesterday evening
on January 18		tomorrow morning
		this evening
		tonight

4 Work in pairs.
  Answer the questions.
  a. Do you know exactly when you were born?
     I was born at two o'clock in the morning on Wednesday, the twenty-fifth of June, 1969.
  b. When did you last go to the cinema / play a sport / give someone a present / have a holiday / watch TV / go to a party / do an exam / see a lot of snow / clean your teeth?
  c. When are you going to leave school / go home / have a holiday / go shopping?

UNIT 4

Going shopping

PRESENTATION

Two friends, Ben and Sam, are going to give a dinner party for their girlfriends.

1 Look below at the ingredients for the main course. Read the recipe, and use your dictionary to check any words you don't know.
2 Work in pairs.
   One of you is Ben and one is Sam.
   Ask each other questions about the ingredients.

How much beef do we need? — 450 grams.

How many onions do we need? — One.

Shepherd's Pie
450g (1 lb) minced beef
1 large onion
2 carrots
50g (2oz) mushrooms
25g (1oz) flour
300 ml (½ pint) beef stock
700g (1½ lb) potatoes
25g (1oz) butter
60ml fresh milk
50g cheese
salt and pepper

● Grammar question

– When do we use **much** and when do we use **many**?

3 ☐ **T.10** ☐ Read and listen to the conversation between Ben and Sam.

Ben	Now, have we got everything we need?
Sam	Well, let's see. There are some onions and potatoes, but there aren't any mushrooms and, of course, there isn't any minced beef.
Ben	Are there any carrots?
Sam	A few. But we don't need many, so that's OK.
Ben	How much milk is there?
Sam	Only a little. And there isn't any butter, and we haven't got much cheese.
Ben	Well, we don't need much cheese. Is there anything else?
Sam	No, not for Shepherd's Pie. We've got some salt and pepper, and there's a lot of flour. Would you like me to help with the shopping?
Ben	Yes, please.

● Grammar questions

Work in pairs.
– Underline with a solid line (_____) all the countable nouns.
– Underline with a broken line (_ _ _ _) all the uncountable nouns.
– Discuss the use of the words in italics in the following sentences.

There *are* some onions.
There *is* some salt.
Are there *any* carrots?
There aren't *any* mushrooms.
There isn't *any* minced beef.
There is *a lot of* flour.
There are *a lot of* potatoes.

– How do we use **a few** and **a little**? **Much** and **many**?

● Language review

Expressions of quantity

Some/any
Some is generally used in positive sentences. **Any** is used in questions and negatives.
*Have we got **any** eggs?*
*There's **some** salt, but there isn't **any** pepper.*

Much/many/a lot of
Much and **many** are generally used in questions and negatives, **much** with uncountable nouns and **many** with countable nouns.
*How **much** money have you got?*
*There aren't **many** parks in my town.*
A lot of is used in positive sentences, with countable and uncountable nouns.
*He's got **a lot of** money.*
*There are **a lot of** parks in London.*

A few/a little
A few is used with countable nouns. **A little** is used with uncountable nouns.
*There are **a few** biscuits in the tin.*
*There's **a little** whisky left. Help yourself.*

PRACTICE

1 Grammar

1 Put **some** or **any** into each gap.
  a. Have you got _____ brothers or sisters?
  b. We don't need _____ butter.
  c. There are _____ books on the table.
  d. I want _____ flour because I'm going to bake a cake.
  e. Is there _____ petrol in the car?

2 Put **much**, **many**, or **a lot of** into each gap.
  a. Have you got _____ homework?
  b. We don't need _____ eggs.
  c. There are _____ dirty plates in the sink.
  d. There is _____ unemployment in my town.
  e. Are there _____ unemployed people in your country?

2 Speaking and writing

1 Here are the ingredients for the dessert that Ben and Sam are going to make. Use your dictionary to check any words you don't know.

Work in pairs
Look at their fridge and cupboard. Ask and answer questions about the ingredients in the recipe.

Is there	any/much . . . ?	Yes, there is/are.
Are there	any/many . . . ?	No, there aren't.
Have they got		Yes, they have.
Do they need	any/many/much . . . ?	No, they don't.

2 Now write the conversation between Ben and Sam as they plan the dessert. Begin like this:

Ben *Have we got everything for the dessert?*
Sam *Well, let's see. . .*

3 Grammar

some		thing
any	+	where
		body
		one

The rules for **something/anything**, etc. are the same as for **some** and **any**.
  ***Someone** phoned you last night.* (positive)
  *We didn't go **anywhere**.* (negative)
  *Did you have **anything** to eat at lunchtime?* (question)

Put one of the combinations into each gap.
  a. 'Did you meet _____ interesting at the party?'
  b. 'Yes, I met _____ who knows you. His name's Alan Clark.'
  c. 'Ouch! There's _____ in my eye!'
  d. 'Let me have a look. I can't see _____ .'
  e. 'Let's go _____ hot for our holiday.'
  f. 'OK. But I don't want to go _____ that's too expensive.'
  g. 'I'm bored! I want _____ interesting to read, or _____ interesting to talk to, or _____ interesting to go!'

27

4 Speaking and listening

What is your favourite dish?
What ingredients do you need to make it?
Don't say how to make it! You're going to do that on page 31. If you want to know how to make Shepherd's Pie or Apple Cake, ask your teacher!

● Language review

Expressions of quantity

> **Translate**
>
> We've got some eggs, but we haven't got any butter.
>
> _____
>
> There are a few apples and a lot of oranges.
>
> _____
>
> There's a little butter and a lot of flour.
>
> _____
>
> There aren't many raisins, and there isn't much sugar.
>
> _____

▶ **Grammar reference: page 123.**

PRESENTATION

Read the following short text and underline all the definite and indefinite articles.

> My uncle is a shopkeeper. He has a shop in a small village by the River Thames near Oxford. The shop sells almost everything from bread to newspapers. It is also the post office. The children always stop to spend a few pence on sweets or ice-cream on their way to and from school. My uncle doesn't often leave the village. He doesn't have a car, so once a month he goes by bus to Oxford and has lunch at the Grand Hotel. He is one of the happiest men I know.

▶ **Grammar reference: page 123.**

Look at the grammar reference.
It gives rules about the use of definite and indefinite articles, and when we use no article.
Find examples of some of the rules in the text above.

PRACTICE

Grammar

1 Work in pairs to find one mistake in each of the following sentences.
   a. He's milkman, so he has breakfast at 4 a.m.
   b. I want a government to do something about the problem of unemployment.
   c. Cities are usually exciting – in London, for example, you can have tea at the Ritz and then go to the theatre in evening.
   d. I must go to a bank and see my bank manager. I want to borrow one hundred pounds.

2 Put **a**, **the**, or _nothing_ into each gap.
   a. I have two children, _____ girl and _____ boy. _____ girl is six and _____ boy is four.
   b. She goes to _____ work in _____ City by _____ train every day. Her office is in _____ Baker Street.
   c. I never read _____ newspapers during the week, but I buy _____ _Observer_ every Sunday and I read it in _____ bed.
   d. When you go to _____ France, you must take _____ boat on _____ Seine when you are in _____ Paris.

● Language review

Articles

> **Translate**
>
> I have breakfast in bed on Sundays.
>
> _____
>
> Love is more important than work.
>
> _____
>
> He's a doctor. He works in Harley Street.
>
> _____

SKILLS DEVELOPMENT

● Reading and speaking

You are going to read a magazine article about one of Britain's most famous shops – Marks & Spencer.

Pre-reading task

Work in pairs and use dictionaries if necessary.

The following people, places, and things are in the article. What connection do you think they have with Marks & Spencer? They appear here in the same order as in the text.

– Princess Diana   – Spain
– £10 million   – Paris and Newcastle
– a Polish immigrant – jumpers
– shoelaces   – chiropodists

Now read the article quickly and discuss the list again.

MARKS & SPENCER

Britain's favourite store

Marks & Spencer (or M&S) is Britain's favourite store. Tourists love it too. It attracts a great variety of customers, from housewives to millionaires. Princess Diana, Dustin Hoffman, and the British
5 Prime Minister are just a few of its famous customers.

Last year it made a profit of £529 million, which is more than £10 million a week.

How did it all begin?

10 It all started 105 years ago, when a young Polish immigrant, Michael Marks, had a stall in Leeds market. He didn't have many things to sell: some cotton, a little wool, lots of buttons, and a few shoelaces. Above his stall he put the now famous
15 notice:

> **DON'T ASK HOW MUCH –
> IT'S A PENNY.**

Ten years later, he met Tom Spencer and together they started Penny Stalls in many towns in the
20 north of England. Today there are 564 branches of M&S all over the world – in America, Canada, Spain, France, Belgium, and Hungary.

What are the best-sellers?

Surprisingly, tastes in food and clothes are
25 international. What sells well in Paris sells just as well in Newcastle. Their best-selling clothes are:

- For women: jumpers, bras, and knickers (M&S is famous for its knickers!).
- For men: shirts, socks, pyjamas, dressing gowns,
30 and suits.
- For children: underwear and socks.

Best-sellers in food include: fresh chickens, bread, vegetables, and sandwiches. Chicken Kiev is internationally the most popular convenience food.

35 ### Why is M&S so successful?

The store bases its business on three principles: good value, good quality, and good service. Also, it changes with the times – once it was all jumpers and knickers. Now it's food, furniture, and flowers
40 as well. Top fashion designers advise on styles of clothes.

But perhaps the most important key to its success is its happy, well-trained staff. Conditions of work are excellent. There are company doctors,
45 dentists, hairdressers, and even chiropodists to look after the staff, and all the staff can have lunch for under 40p!

Comprehension check
Here are some answers. What are the questions?

1 _____
  £529 million.
2 _____
  105 years ago.
3 _____
  Poland.
4 _____
  No, he only had a few things.
5 _____
  564.
6 _____
  Because it gives good value, good quality, and good service.
7 _____
  No, it doesn't. It sells food and furniture as well.
8 _____
  Less than 40p.

Vocabulary work
In the text there are a lot of examples of clothes, food, and professions. List them in the columns below and add three more examples of your own to each column.

Clothes	Food	Professions

Now check all the examples in your class. How many different examples do you have?

Speaking
Here are the four headings from the text.

Britain's favourite store

How did it all begin?

What are the best-sellers?

Why is M&S so successful?

1 Use these to help you say in a few words the main points of the text.
2 Use the headings to help you to talk about one of the favourite stores in your country.

● **Vocabulary**

Food and cooking

1 Look at the pictures of vegetables, fruit, and meat. Use your bilingual dictionary to find the English names of those you don't know. Write the English word under each picture.

2 The following verbs are for preparing and cooking food. Which often go with the food in the pictures above?

bake	boil	chop	cut	fry	grill
peel	roast	slice	squeeze		

Can you think of other food words that often go with these verbs?

Listening and speaking

Five radio advertisements

Pre-listening task

1 Is there an advertisement on the television or in the newspapers at the moment that you particularly like? What's it for?

2 Read the definitions of the following words.

> **break** (*n*) a rest; an advertisement on radio or television
> **fair** (*n*) a large exhibition of commercial goods, e.g. a book/motor fair

> **ferry** (*n*) a boat that carries people and/or cars across rivers and seas
> **grown-up** (*n*) an adult
> **kid** (*n*) another word for a child

3 Work in groups.
Imagine you work in advertising. How can you sell the following things? What information will you give about them in the advertisement?
   – a soft drink
   – a musical at the theatre
   – a cross-Channel ferry
   – a new kind of frozen
      potato dish
   – a motor fair
Compare your suggestions.

Listening for information

T.11 You will hear five radio advertisements. They are for the things you talked about in question **3** above, but not in the same order.
Listen to them, and say what each one is for.

The first one is an advertisement for . . .

Comprehension check
Try to answer the following questions. Then listen to the advertisements again.
1 What is the name of the food in the first advertisement?
2 What is the name of the ferry company?
3 What is the name of the musical?
4 When does the motor fair end?
5 What is the name of the soft drink?
6 How do you cook Oven Crunchies?
7 How much is a day-trip from Dover?
8 Where can you get tickets for the musical?
9 What are some of the extras the man wanted in his Cadillac?
10 What can you get when you buy Coca-Cola?

Group work
Work in groups of four.
Think of a radio advertisement to make people come to a private English language school. What information will you give (prices, location, best teachers)? Will the advertisement have a story (*Before I came to this school, my English was terrible, but now . . .*)?

3 Here is some of the kitchen equipment used to prepare or cook food.

> bowl   frying pan   saucepan
> casserole dish   knife   oven   wok

Write down the instructions for your favourite recipe.

Example
Peel and chop the onions and fry them in a saucepan. Next, . . .

● Everyday English

Polite requests and offers

1 Match a line in **A** with a line in **B**.

The people are in one of the following places.

baker's	department store	post office
airport	railway station	supermarket
chemist's	fast food restaurant	

Where are they?

A	B
1 Can I have a book of stamps, please?	a. Yes, of course. It's on the third floor.
2 We'd like two cheeseburgers and one Big Mac, all with fries, please.	b. Do you want first class or second?
	c. I'll check, but I think we only have it for dry.
3 Could you tell me where the shoe department is, please?	d. Yes, that's fine. I'll give you a label for it.
4 Have you got any Sunsilk shampoo for greasy hair?	e. Would you like anything to drink with that?
5 Excuse me. Can you tell me where platform six is?	f. Here you are. We don't charge for them.
6 I'd like a large, brown, sliced loaf, please.	g. It's over there. Come with me. I'll show you.
7 Can I take this bag as hand luggage?	h. I'm afraid we only have white left.
8 Could I have another plastic bag? I've got so much to carry.	

2 **T.12** Listen and check your answers. Listen carefully to the intonation of the requests, and practise saying them.

3 Underline the different structures that express a polite request in **A**. There are three offers in **B**. Find them. What verb form is used for making offers?

▶ Grammar reference: page 124.

4 Work in pairs.
Write similar dialogues for some of the following places.

newsagent's	bookshop	butcher's
tourist office	cinema	greengrocer's
hotel	clothes shop	bank

UNIT 5

Verb patterns (1) – Going to – Will – Spelling

Plans and ambitions

PRESENTATION

1 Read the texts about these three people. They are talking about what they want to do in life.
Who knows what he/she wants to do? Who isn't sure?

Pippa Wilson is studying marketing at university. She enjoys travelling, and would probably like to work for a tour company. 'I'm not sure yet exactly what I want to do. After university, I'm going to have a year off, and I'm going round the world with another girl. We hope to find work on the way.'

Angela Duffy is a schoolgirl from Brighton. She wants to be a doctor. 'I'm going to medical school next year. It's a long course – about six years – but I'm going to work very hard. It's a difficult job, but I like working with people, and I like the idea of working in a caring profession.' She says that later she would like to specialize and perhaps be a paediatrician. 'I love children, and looking after them would be wonderful.'

Steve Barnes wants to be a chef. His favourite room in the house is the kitchen, where he spends most of the day. 'I love cooking, especially for lots of people. I have over a hundred cook books.'
He's going to work in a restaurant in Paris, where he hopes to learn how to prepare sauces. 'English people really don't know how to cook imaginatively,' he says, 'but we have the best ingredients in the world. One day I'd like to have my own restaurant.'

2 Fill in the chart about the three people.

	Ambition(s)	Reason(s)	What is he/she going to do?
Angela			
Steve			
Pippa			

● Grammar questions

– Underline the verb forms in the texts that express plans and ambitions.

  wants to be *a doctor*

– Underline the correct verb form in the following sentences.

  I would like *be/being/to be* a doctor.
  He's going *to work/work/working* in a restaurant in Paris.
  She hopes *find/to find* a job soon.
  He wants *have/to have* a restaurant.

– What's the difference in meaning between the verb forms in the following two sentences?

  I *like working* with children.
  I'*d like to be* a paediatrician.

33

PRACTICE

1 Speaking

Work in pairs.
What do the following people want to do?
What are they going to do?

Example
John thinks his job is boring. (He likes acting.)
He wants to find another job.
He'd like to work in the theatre.
He's going (to go) to drama school.
He hopes to be famous one day.

a. Peter and Janet are planning their winter holiday. (They like skiing.)
b. Ruth doesn't like living in the centre of town any more.
c. Alice is looking at advertisements for second-hand cars (but she doesn't have any money).
d. Jorge (from Madrid) is studying hotel management. He's also learning English.
e. Clara (aged 15) is a brilliant tennis player. She practises every day.
f. Joanna (from England) is doing a course to train to be an English language teacher. (She loves South America.)
g. David and Beth are very much in love.

2 Grammar

Complete the following sentences using a form of **would like** (to do) or **like** (doing). Put the verbs in brackets in the correct form, too.

a. There's a good film on at the Odeon Cinema. _____ you _____ (see) it with me?
b. I'm thirsty. I _____ something to drink.
c. 'Who is your favourite painter?'
   'I _____ all the Impressionists, especially Monet.'
d. 'Do you do any sport?'
   'Yes. I _____ (swim) and _____ (play) football.'
e. She's learning Italian because she _____ (go) to Italy on holiday next year.
f. ' _____ you _____ (learn) English?'
   'Yes, but sometimes I find it a bit difficult.'

3 Speaking and listening

Work in pairs.
Ask and answer questions about your plans and ambitions.

> Which countries would you like to go to?
> When . . . get married?
> How many children . . .?
> What . . . after this course?
> . . . have your own business?

> I'd like to . . .
> I want to . . .
> I'm going to . . .

● Language review

Verb patterns

It is very common for one verb to be followed by another verb. When this happens, the second verb can have different patterns. Two possible patterns are the infinitive and the **-ing** form.

Infinitive		**-ing forms**	
I want		*I like*	
I'd like	*to be a doctor.*	*I love*	*cooking.*
I hope		*I enjoy*	
I'm going			

There is a list of verb patterns on page 143.

Like doing/would like to do

Like doing expresses a general enjoyment or preference.
Would like to do expresses a preference now, or at a specific time.

Translate

I like swimming.

_____

I'm tired. I'd like to go to bed.

_____

I'd like to buy a new car next year.

_____

▶ Grammar reference: page 124.

PRESENTATION

1 Jenny and Chris are talking about their plans for next week. Read their conversation and put a form of **going** (to) or **will** into each gap.

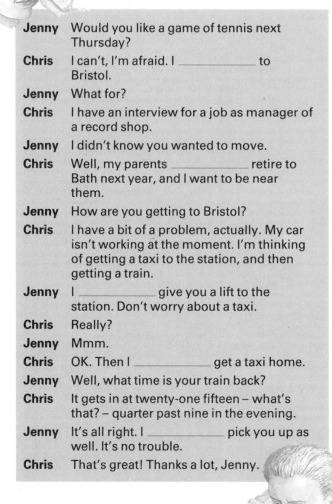

Jenny	Would you like a game of tennis next Thursday?
Chris	I can't, I'm afraid. I _____ to Bristol.
Jenny	What for?
Chris	I have an interview for a job as manager of a record shop.
Jenny	I didn't know you wanted to move.
Chris	Well, my parents _____ retire to Bath next year, and I want to be near them.
Jenny	How are you getting to Bristol?
Chris	I have a bit of a problem, actually. My car isn't working at the moment. I'm thinking of getting a taxi to the station, and then getting a train.
Jenny	I _____ give you a lift to the station. Don't worry about a taxi.
Chris	Really?
Jenny	Mmm.
Chris	OK. Then I _____ get a taxi home.
Jenny	Well, what time is your train back?
Chris	It gets in at twenty-one fifteen – what's that? – quarter past nine in the evening.
Jenny	It's all right. I _____ pick you up as well. It's no trouble.
Chris	That's great! Thanks a lot, Jenny.

2 [**T.13**] Listen to the complete conversation and check your answers.

● Grammar questions

– When did Chris decide to go to Bristol? *Before* he spoke to Jenny or *while* he was speaking to her?
– When did Jenny decide to give Chris a lift? *Before* she spoke to Chris or *while* she was speaking to him?
– What's the difference between **going to** and **will** to express a future intention?

PRACTICE

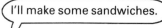

1 Speaking and listening

1 Your class has decided to have a party. Everyone must help to prepare for it. Say what you'll do.

> I'll make some sandwiches.

> I'll buy some bread.

2 Your teacher didn't hear what you said! Listen to your teacher, and correct him or her.

Teacher	**You**
OK. I'll make some sandwiches.	No, *I'm going to* make them!
All right. Well, I'll buy some bread.	No, *I'm going to* buy it!

2 Grammar

Work in pairs to decide which is the correct verb form.
a. 'My suitcase is so heavy!'
   'Give it to me. *I'll/I'm going to* carry it for you.'
b. I bought some warm boots because *I'll go/I'm going* skiing.
c. 'Tony's back from holiday.'
   'Is he? *I'll give/I'm going to give* him a ring.'
d. *We'll see/We're going to see* 'Hamlet' at the Royal Shakespeare tonight. The tickets were very expensive.
e. You can tell me your secret. *I won't tell/I'm not going to tell* anyone else.
f. I hear you and John *will get/are going to get* married! Congratulations!
g. 'I need to get these letters in the post as soon as possible.'
   '*I'll go/I'm going* shopping soon. *I'll post/I'm going to post* them for you.'
h. 'Where *will you go/are you going* on holiday this year?'
   'Turkey. What about you?'
   'We don't know yet. Maybe *we will go/we are going to Spain*.'

3 Speaking and listening

In pairs, ask and answer questions about your plans for tonight, next weekend, and your next holiday.

> What are you doing/ going to do tonight? Where are you going …?

> I'm going to see a film/stay at home and …

● Language review

Going to

Going to is used to express a future intention thought about before the moment of speaking.

> **Translate**
>
> We are going to get married next spring.
>
> _____

Will

Will is used to express a future intention or decision made at the moment of speaking.

> **Translate**
>
> Give me your case. I'll carry it for you.
>
> _____

Other uses of **will** are in Unit 9.

▶ **Grammar reference: page 124.**

SKILLS DEVELOPMENT

● Reading and speaking

How ambitious are you?

1 Answer the questions from the questionnaire below and add up your score to find out how ambitious you are! Use your dictionary if necessary.
2 Do you agree with the interpretations?
3 Choose one of the questions.
   Stand up and ask all the other students your question. Then report back to the class.

Everybody thinks . . .
Nobody wants . . .
Most of us would like. . .
Some people hope . . . but others don't want. . .

How ambitious are you?

1 In ten years do you hope to
 a be married with a family?
 b have an interesting but not very well-paid job?
 c have a well-paid job that isn't very interesting?

2 In twenty years' time do you hope to
 a have enough money to pay your bills?
 b have quite a lot of money?
 c have a lot of money?

3 Here is a list of ten jobs. Which would you like to do? Put 1 next to your favourite, 2 next to your next favourite, etc.
 nurse   builder
 accountant   journalist
 teacher   artist
 politician   engineer
 policeman/woman
 actor/actress/pop star

4 Is improving your standard of living important to you?

5 Do you think people who have money should help people who don't have money?

6 How old do you want to be when you have children?
 a 18 – 22   b 23 – 26
 c 27 – 30   d over 30

7 When you are playing a game, do you always want to win?

8 Can you tell a white lie?

9 Do you think that rich people are happier and more interesting than other people?

10 Do you work hard because you want to be successful?

11 If you have a job to do, do you do it immediately, or do you wait until the last moment?

12 Would you like to have more money than your parents?

13 Do you agree with the philosophy 'Every man for himself'?

14 Do you like hard work?

15 Which of the following is most important to you?

 love happiness money health

Answers

1 a 0   b 5   c 10
2 a 0   b 5   c 10
3 0 nurse/artist first
   2 builder/policeman or policewoman/ teacher/journalist first
   5 engineer/actor/actress/pop star first
   10 politician/accountant first
4 Yes 10 No 0
5 Yes 0   No 10
6 a 0   b 2   c 5   d 10
7 Yes 10 No 0
8 Yes 10 No 0
9 Yes 10 No 0
10 Yes 10 No 0
11 Immediately 10   Last moment 0
12 Yes 10 No 0
13 Yes 10 No 0
14 Yes 10 No 0
15 Love 0   Happiness 5
   Money 10 Health 0

0 – 50 You aren't very ambitious! You're happy with a quiet life.

50 – 100 You're quite ambitious, but you don't want to work too hard!

Over 100 You're very ambitious! Good luck, and try to be nice to people . . .

● Vocabulary and listening

How to learn vocabulary

1 **T.14** You will hear eight learners of English talking about what they do to learn vocabulary. Listen to them and make notes.

2 Work in groups. Have you got a bilingual dictionary? Have you got an English-English dictionary?

3 Choose one of the ideas you heard described. Try it for a week. Then try another one! Tell each other which one you've chosen.

> I'm going to buy a little address book.

Word families

1 The last student described how she looked words up in her dictionary to find word families.
Look at the dictionary extract. Notice how it shows you where the stress is. /'/ means the following syllable is stressed.

> **photo** /'fəʊtəʊ/, **photograph** /'fəʊtəɡrɑːf/ *n.* picture that you make with a camera. **photograph** *v.*: *She photographed the bride and groom outside* the church. **photographer** /fə'tɒɡrəfə(r)/ *n.* someone who takes pictures with a camera. **photography** /fə'tɒɡrəfɪ/ *n.* **photographic** /fəʊtə'ɡræfɪk/ *adj.*

Practise saying the words in the dictionary entry. How does *your* dictionary show where the stress is?

2 The following suffixes are used to form different parts of speech.

nouns	-ment	-ness	-sion	-tion	-ty	-al
adjectives	-ful	-ic	-able	-ous	-y	-ive
	-al					
verbs	-ize/ise					

The words in the charts below have all appeared in Units 1–5 of *Headway Pre-Intermediate*. Use your dictionary to find the other parts of speech, and mark the stress. The suffixes in exercise **2** are used (but not always!).

Noun	Adjective	Noun	Verb
am'bition			im'prove
	'happy		a'rrive
'power		'government	
			de'cide
'science			e'lect
tech'nology		organi'zation	
'health		com'plaint	
'person			i'magine
'fashion			in'vite
			de'scribe
			em'ploy

Noun	Verb	Adjective
suc'cess		
a'ttraction		
		'special
natio'nality		

3 What is special about the nouns and verbs of the following words?

change	cook	light	interview
question	dream	drink	

● Reading and speaking

The right person for you

Pre-reading task

A dating agency is an organization that tries to find a partner (a boyfriend or girlfriend) for someone to go out with. Are there dating agencies in your country? What are they called? How do they work?

Vocabulary

Match a line in **A** with a line in **B** to define the words in italics. Use your dictionary if you want.

A	B
If you are *desperate* for something,	one that is important and well paid.
If you are *seeking* something,	you have a good relationship.
	you are looking for it.
A *high-flier* is	a TV programme that gives factual information about something.
A *high-powered* job is	the qualification you get from university.
A *documentary* is	someone who is ambitious.
If you *get on well* with someone,	someone who is kind, and pays attention to other people's feelings.
A *degree* is	you want it very, very much, and will do anything to get it.
If you are *fed up* with something,	you are unhappy or bored with it.
A *considerate* person is	

Jigsaw reading

1 You will now read an article from the *Today* newspaper.
   Look at the headline and the introduction.
   What sort of people is the article about?
   Why are they going to dating agencies?
2 Divide into two groups.
   Group A Read about the American, John Frantz.
   Group B Read about the English woman, Nicolette Morganti.
   Answer the comprehension check questions as you read.

Comprehension check

1 What is his/her job?
2 Is it a good job?
3 Does he/she own a house?
4 Where does he/she want to live?
5 What sort of person does he/she want to meet?
6 What sort of person doesn't he/she like?
7 Does he/she want to have children?
8 Who has he/she met already?
9 Was it a successful meeting?
10 What is he/she going to do?

DESPERATELY SEEKING SOMEONE

THE LONELY HIGH FLIERS TRYING TO FIND LOVE

THEY have money, good looks and high-powered jobs, but in the fight to the top they forgot one thing – finding a partner.

Now over 30, they have no time to start looking. As a result, more and more lonely single people are asking others to help them find love. According to 'Desperately Seeking Someone', a four-part BBC documentary starting soon, dating agencies, social clubs, and small advertisements in magazines are becoming a multi-million pound business.

Today reporter Margaret Morrison spoke to some of the lonely hearts who told her about just who you meet when you pay for the introduction.

My girl must like me, not my wallet

JOHN FRANTZ 36
Divorced (Sales Manager)

'US girls want cash'

AMERICAN John Frantz has a wonderful lifestyle and he wants to share it with an English girl.

5   At 36, he's the national sales manager for a big printing firm, earns £65,000-plus and drives a grey Cadillac. Home
10 is a six-bedroom, five bathroom mansion in 1½ acres of land near Washington DC.

'I want to stay in this house,' says John. 'I like exotic holidays, but I wouldn't like to
15 live outside the US.' Divorced five years ago, he now hopes to find a wife with the English Rose dating agency in Kent.

'Children aren't so
20 important to me. I don't want to go to bars to meet women because in the US they are more interested in your wallet,' he says. 'I meet a lot of
25 people through work, but I've got a strict rule of never dating women colleagues.

'I know a couple of British women at home and they have
30 an air of independence that US women don't have. I'd like to meet someone who's intelligent and who has her own opinions.' His first
35 transatlantic phone call came from Sandy, a secretary living in Middlesex.

'We exchanged photo-

When you have answered your questions, find a partner from the other group.
Compare your answers and swap information.

38

...raphs, but when she called ...here was a bit of a language ...roblem. We didn't understand ...ach other's accent! After that 45 ...ve got on well. I decided to ...ome over to London for 12 ...ays.

'We went out for lunch and dinner a couple of times, and we're going sightseeing on Saturday.

50 'I'd like to see more of her but romance takes a while to develop. There are a couple of other women I'm going to see while I'm here.'

Nicky wants to be your English rose

NICOLETTE MORGANTI 29, Single (News agency PA)

'I want a husband'

...ICOLETTE Morganti's ...iends can't understand why she ...oined a dating agency.

She has a good job as a per- ...onal assistant with a television ...ews agency, her own home, ...nd a full social life. But the 29- ...ear-old, who has a degree in ...nglish Literature, is so fed up ...ith British men that she joined ...ne English Rose dating agency ...o get in touch with single ...American males.

'English men are usually ...aterialistic and have no imagi- ...ation,' she says. 'I have spent ...ears being bored by men who ...ever do anything exciting.'

'I'm almost 30 now and I ...ould really love to find a hus- ...and and have children. I'd like ...o live in London for six months ...f the year and in the States for ...he other six months.'

In her search for the ideal man, ...icolette once put an advertise- ...ment in a magazine for single ...eople and had 400 replies.

But she says: 'I only met one 30 or two of them. Most of the others sounded very boring.'

Nicolette joined English Rose about 18 months ago and has 35 met 5 men since then.

She says: 'I find that Ameri- can men are more romantic and considerate than British men. I rang one in the States, and after- wards he sent me 200 dollars to 40 pay for the call.

'I've met five so far but I'm looking for someone very special. I'd like to find a caring, well-educated, non-smoking 45 animal-lover with a professional job and a sense of adventure.'

Nicolette is going to stay with English Rose until she finds her man.

50 'My friends have said some horrible things, but I think it's a great way to meet people.'

What do you think?
1 Do you think John and Nicolette would get on if they met each other? Why/why not?
2 In your country, where do teenagers go when they want to go out in the evening? What about young adults?
3 In many countries, marriages are arranged by the parents. If you come from one of these countries, do you think arranged marriages are a good idea?
If you come from a country where marriages are *not* arranged, would you like your parents to find a partner for you?

● **Everyday English**

Spelling

1 Practise saying the letters of the alphabet according to the vowel sounds.

/eɪ/	/iː/	/e/	/aɪ/	/əʊ/	/uː/	/ɑː/
a	b	f	i	o	q	r
h	c	l	y		u	
j	d	m			w	
k	e	n				
	g	s				
	p	x				
	t	z				
	v					

2 Learners of English can find some of the letters difficult.
Try to remember the following:
   '*e*' *is easy, and rhymes with* **tea**.
   '*i*' *is like* 👁, *and rhymes with* **my**.
   '*a*' *rhymes with* **day**, **way**, **May**, *and* **say**.
   For '*j*', *think of* **Jane**.
   For '*g*', *think of Einstein, who was a* **genius**.
   '*r*' *is what the doctor tells you to say!*
   '*y*' *is like the question* **Why?**
   '*h*' *is like the sound in* **nature**.

3 **T.15** You will hear a man called Henry telling you the names of the members of his family.
Write them on the family tree.

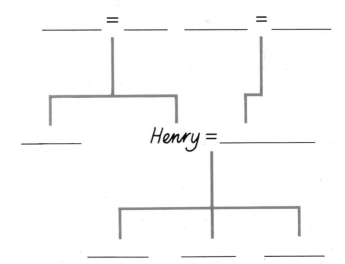

4 Work in pairs.
Dictate to each other the names of the members of your family, and also your address.
You will have to help with the spelling sometimes!

Examples
'*d*' *for Daddy!*
'*s*' *for sugar!*
'*r*' *for red!*

39

UNIT 6

Descriptions

PRESENTATION

Tina Stanley is a violinist with the London Festival Orchestra. She lives in London but she travels all over the world with the orchestra. Last year she visited New York, Tokyo, and Rome.

T.16a Listen to what she says to a friend about these cities. Write down the adjectives she uses.

New York:

Tokyo:

Rome:

Grammar questions

Her friend asks Tina about her tour last year.
She says: *Tell me about Rome.* **What's it like?**
– Is she asking if Tina likes the places she visited?
– Is she asking Tina to describe the places she visited?

PRACTICE

1 Grammar

1 Work in pairs.
  Ask and answer questions about the places Tina visited.

  What's ... like?

  It's (It is) ...
  It's (It has) got ...

2 Tina's friend asked her some more questions about New York. Complete the questions using *What is/are ... like?*

  a. **Friend** What _____ like?
     Tina It's cold in winter and hot in summer.

  b. **Friend** What _____ like?
     Tina Well, they're interesting, but they can be a bit rude.

  c. **Friend** What _____ like?
     Tina It's wonderful. You can find food from every country in the world.

  d. **Friend** What _____ like?
     Tina They're very modern and very, very tall. Some of them are sixty floors high.

  e. **Friend** What _____ like?
     Tina They're open all the time, and you can buy everything you need.

40

2 Speaking and listening

Ask and answer questions about your last holiday.

> Where did you go?
> What was the weather like?
> Where . . . stay?
> What was the (hotel) like?
> . . . food . . . ?
> . . . beaches . . . ?

● Language review

Asking for descriptions

What . . . like? asks for a general description of people, places, or things.

*'**What**'s London **like**?'*
'It's big and noisy, with a lot of parks.'
*'**What**'s Emma **like**?'*
'She's very nice, very intelligent, and pretty.'

Here, **like** is a preposition. Don't confuse it with **like** used as a verb (*I **like** Coke. / Do you **like** swimming?*).

Translate	
'What's your sister like?'	'She's pretty and intelligent.'
'What does your sister like?'	'She likes chocolate and ice-cream.'

▶ **Grammar reference: page 125.**

PRESENTATION

1 ☐ **T.16b** ☐ Listen to the second part of the conversation with Tina. She compares the cities. Notice the words she uses to do this.

2 Comparative and superlative adjectives are formed in three ways.
1 with **-er** and **-est**
2 with **-ier** and **-iest**
3 with **more** and **most**
What are the comparative and superlative forms of the following adjectives? Put 1, 2, or 3 next to each one.
(**Good** and **bad** are irregular!)

beautiful ___	cold ___	old ___
ugly ___	hot ___	near ___
big ___	crowded ___	far (irreg) ___
small ___	exciting ___	noisy ___
busy ___	friendly ___	quiet ___
cheap ___	heavy ___	polluted ___
expensive ___	interesting ___	wet ___
clean ___	boring ___	dry ___
dirty ___	modern ___	good/bad (irreg)

● Grammar question

– When do you use **-er/-est**, **-ier/-iest**, and **more/most**?

3 Here are some of the things Tina said about the cities she visited. Some are facts and some are her opinions. Complete her sentences.
a. Tokyo's exciting, but, for a musician, London is _____ exciting _____ Tokyo, and, of course, New York is _____ _____ exciting of all.
b. London is, of course, much older _____ New York, but it isn't _____ old _____ Rome. Rome is _____ oldest city I visited.

c. London doesn't have _____ many old buildings _____ Rome, but it has _____ _____ both New York and Tokyo.
d. New York has _____ parks than Tokyo, but London has _____ _____ parks. There are five in the city centre.
Listen again and check your answers.

41

4 | T.16c | Listen to this sentence on the tape.

London ͜ is ͜ older than New York,
but ͜ it ͜ isn't ͜ as ͜ old ͜ as Rome.

Notice that **than** and **as** are weak and are pronounced /ðən/ and /əz/. Notice also that there are many word links.

Work in pairs.
Practise saying the following sentences, paying attention to weak forms and word links. Then listen to the rest of the exercise and repeat.

I'm not as tall as you.
But I'm taller than Ann.

It's not as cold today as it was yesterday.
But it's colder than it was last week.

This book is more interesting than I thought.
But it isn't as interesting as the one I read last week.

PRACTICE

1 Grammar

Work in pairs to correct the following sentences.
a. He's more older than he looks.
b. Ann's as tall than her mother.
c. 'What does Paris like?'
   'It's beautiful, especially in the spring.'
d. Concorde is the most fast passenger plane in the world.
e. Trains in Tokyo are crowdeder than in London.
f. Oxford is one of oldest universities in Europe.
g. He isn't as intelligent than his sister.
h. This is more hard than I expected.
i. Who is the most rich man in the world?
j. Everything is more cheap in my country.

2 Speaking

Work in pairs.
Continue one of the following conversations.

A I've got a new car.
B Oh, really? What's it like?
A Well, it's faster than my old car, so it isn't as economical, but . . .

A I moved house last week.
B Oh, really? What's the new house like?
A Well, . . .

A You know John/Julia and I broke up recently – well, I met a very nice boy/girl last night.
B Oh, really? What's he/she like?
A Well, . . .

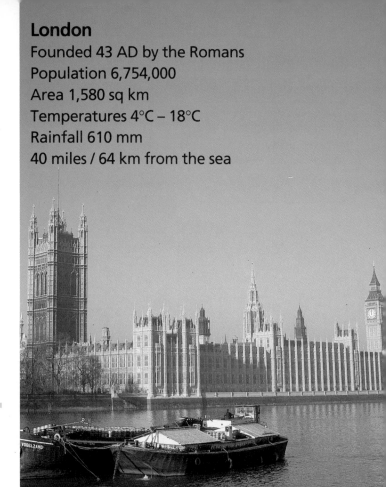

London
Founded 43 AD by the Romans
Population 6,754,000
Area 1,580 sq km
Temperatures 4°C – 18°C
Rainfall 610 mm
40 miles / 64 km from the sea

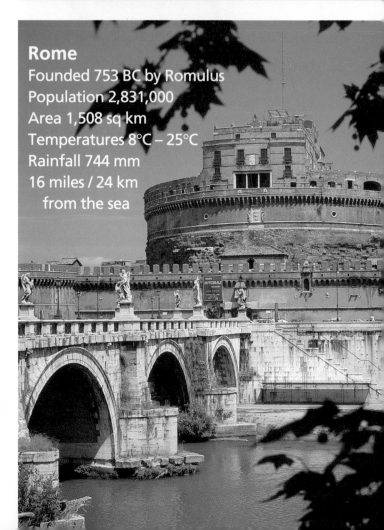

Rome
Founded 753 BC by Romulus
Population 2,831,000
Area 1,508 sq km
Temperatures 8°C – 25°C
Rainfall 744 mm
16 miles / 24 km
    from the sea

Tokyo
Founded 1456 AD as Edo
Population 11,807,000
Area 1,250 sq km
Temperatures 3°C – 26°C
Rainfall 1,563 mm
On the Pacific coast

New York
Founded 1609 AD as New
    Amsterdam
Population 7,071,639
Area 956 sq km
Temperatures -1°C – 23°C
Rainfall 1,123 mm
On the Atlantic coast

3 Speaking and writing

Look at the facts about London, New York, Rome, and Tokyo. Use the information to make comparisons between the cities with **-er/more** . . . **than**; **not as** . . . **as**; **the -est/most** . . .

Write down some of your sentences. Do you know other things about these cities? What is your opinion of them? Make more comparisons. Use the box of adjectives on page 41 to help you.

4 Speaking and listening

Work in groups of three.
If you live in the same town, *either* compare facts and opinions about the different parts of town, *or* compare different parts of your country.
If you come from different towns, describe them to each other, and then compare them.

What's your town like?

It's quite modern and big. It has a population of about 200,000.

My town's (much) smaller than that.

● Language review

Comparatives and superlatives

Adjectives have a comparative and superlative form. Adjectives also combine with **as** . . . **as** to express equality, and **not as/so** . . . **as** to express inequality.

Translate

I'm older than you.

Peter's the tallest in the class.

Your car is as big as mine.

But my house isn't as big as yours.

▶ **Grammar reference: page 125.**

SKILLS DEVELOPMENT

● Reading and speaking

You are going to read a newspaper article about the Sultan of Brunei. He is the richest man in the world.

Pre-reading task

1 Have you heard of the country of Brunei?
Do you know where it is?
Is it in the Middle East/East Asia/West Africa?

2 Check in your dictionary that you understand the following words:

extravagant (*adj*)   **shy** (*adj*)
wealth (*n*)/**wealthy** (*adj*)   **reserved** (*adj*) e.g. a
chandelier (*n*)   reserved person
despite (*prep*)   **outgoing** (*adj*) e.g. an
to share (*v*)   outgoing person

Reading for information

Now read the article quite quickly. As you read, check if you were right about where Brunei is.
Decide what you think is the most extravagant way the Sultan spends his money. Discuss your ideas in pairs.

THE RICHEST MAN IN THE WORLD

A year ago the Sultan of Brunei gave a birthday party for his eleven-year-old daughter. It was in the ballroom of Claridges Hotel, in Mayfair, London. It cost
5 £100,000, but for the Sultan this is not a great amount of money. He is so rich that he can buy whatever he wants.

A few years ago he built the
10 biggest palace in the world. It has 1,788 rooms, 5 swimming pools, 257 toilets, 44 staircases and 18 lifts. The dining room can seat 4,000 people. There are 564
15 chandeliers with 51,490 light bulbs. A servant is employed full time to change bulbs – about 200 a day. The total cost of the palace was $400 million. The Sultan invited
20 his friends to see it but they didn't like it – they said it looked more like a multi-storey car park than a palace. What could the Sultan do? You guessed – he built another
25 one!

Brunei is one of the smallest but richest countries in the world. Its wealth comes from oil and gas. Most people think that Brunei is in the Middle East but it isn't. It's in East Asia, on the north coast of the island of Borneo. It sells
30 the oil and gas to Japan, and earns $2 billion a year – that is $229,000 every hour – from it. And the beauty is that there are so few people to share all this money. The population of Brunei is only 230,000. The Sultan and his brothers are the government.

35 Despite all this money and power the Sultan is a very shy man. He is 42 years old but still looks like a schoolboy. He says very little at international meetings. When he was nineteen he married his cousin, Princess Saleha, who
40 was then sweet, pretty, and only sixteen. Time passed and she became more and more reserved. In 1980 the Sultan met an air hostess
45 called Mariam Bell, who is half Bruneian, a quarter Japanese, and a quarter English. She is much more outgoing in her manner than
50 most Bruneian girls, and the Sultan fell in love with her. He married her, too, and now has two wives and two families all living happily
55 together in the new palace. The Sultan's total wealth is more than $25 billion. He owns hotels all round the world: the Dorchester in
60 London, the Beverley Hills Hotel in Los Angeles and the Hyatt Hotel in Singapore. He has a fleet of private planes, including an airbus. One of his London houses has the biggest garden in the city, except for Buckingham Palace. With all this, is he a happy
65 man? Nobody asks him that.

Comprehension check

1 How many hotels are mentioned in the article? Why are they mentioned?
2 What do the following numbers refer to?
  1,788 257 4,000 200 229,000   230,000 19
  Make a sentence about each number.
3 Find three reasons why Brunei is so rich.
4 Mark Brunei on this map.

5 What is the Sultan like?
6 What are his wives like?
7 Read this summary of the article. There are five mistakes in it. Find them and correct them.

> The Sultan of Brunei spends his great wealth in many ways. For example, he gave a party for his daughter at Claridges, one of the hotels he owns in London. The party cost £100,000. He built two palaces and a multi-storey car park for his guests' cars. He has a few houses in London, and one of them has the biggest garden in the city.
>
> He divorced his first wife and married an air hostess. His first wife now lives in Japan. Brunei is a rich country because it has a lot of oil and gas and can sell it to Japan.

Discussion

Who are the richest people in your country?
Where did their money come from?
How do they spend their money?

● Vocabulary

Synonyms

We often use synonyms in conversation because we don't want to repeat words.

> It's a lovely day today!

> Yes, it's really beautiful.

1 Complete the following conversations using an adjective of similar meaning from the box below.

annoyed	fed up	generous	handsome
marvellous	messy	modern	wealthy

a. 'Mary's family is very rich.'
   'Well, I knew her uncle was _____.'
b. 'Look at all these new buildings!'
   'Yes. The city's much more _____ than I expected.'
c. 'Her boyfriend's really good-looking.'
   'Well, he's certainly one of the most _____ men in the room!'
d. 'Wasn't that film wonderful!'
   'Yes, it was _____.'
e. 'George doesn't earn much money, but he's so kind.'
   'I know. He's very _____ to both his family and his friends.'
f. 'Her bedroom's really untidy again!'
   'Is it? I told her it was _____ yesterday, and she promised to clean it.'
g. 'Was Sara angry when you told her?'
   'Yes. She looked really _____.'
h. 'I'm bored with this lesson!'
   'I know, I'm really _____ with it, too!'

2 **T.17** Listen and check your answers.
Listen again, paying particular attention to the stress and intonation. In pairs, practise saying the dialogues.

Antonyms

We can also use antonyms in conversation to avoid repeating words.

> What an awful meal!

> Yes, it wasn't very nice, was it?

1 Match the following adjectives with their two opposites in the previous exercise.

awful   _____ _____
interested _____ _____
mean   _____ _____
old   _____ _____
poor   _____ _____
pleased   _____ _____
tidy   _____ _____
ugly   _____

45

2 Sometimes we try to be polite by not using a negative adjective, but using **not very** + the opposite.

> Tom's short.

> He's certainly not very tall.

> She always wears dirty clothes.

> Yes, they aren't very clean, are they?

Write in **B**'s answers, and try to be more polite than **A**.

A	B
a. John's so mean.	
b. Rome's an expensive city.	
c. Her house is always messy.	
d. He looks miserable.	
e. His sister's stupid.	
f. The children were naughty today.	
g. The shop assistant was so rude.	

3 You can form the opposite of some adjectives by adding a prefix.

tidy → *untidy*

Choose **un-**, **in-**, or **im-** to form the opposites of the following adjectives.

possible	interested	happy	expensive
friendly	employed	patient	comfortable
polite	important	convenient	correct

Listening

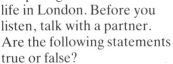

Pre-listening task

You will hear Kate Leigh, an English teacher in Madrid, comparing life in Madrid with life in London. Before you listen, talk with a partner. Are the following statements true or false?

1 In Madrid, people start work early.
2 They finish work at eight in the evening.
3 The shops close for several hours in the middle of the day.
4 People always have a siesta.
5 They don't eat much during the day.
6 They have their main meal in the evening.
7 Madrid is bigger than London.
8 It has no traffic problems.
9 The public transport system is good.

Listening

T.18 Listen to the interview and check your answers to the true/false questions.

Comprehension check

Listen to the interview again, and make a note of some of the comparisons that Kate makes between Madrid and London. These headings will help:

- The time of day that things happen
- Food
- People
- Where people live
- Cost of living
- Shops
- Safety
- Driving
- Public transport
- Weather

What do you think?

Compare Madrid and your town, using the above headings. (If you live in Madrid, compare it with another town!)

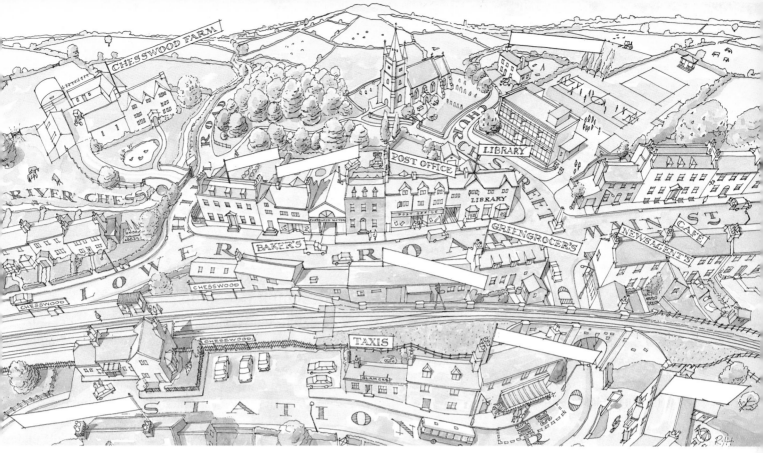

● Everyday English

Directions

Look at the picture of the small town of Chesswood.

1 Find the following things in the picture:

| a farm | a pond | a hill | a railway bridge |
| a wood | a path | a river | a gate |

2 Some of the buildings have not been named.
Read the descriptions of where each building is and write it on the picture.

  a. The hotel is *opposite* the station.
  b. The bank is *on the corner of* Lower Road and Hill Road. It is *next to* the chemist's.
  c. The supermarket is *between* the baker's and the greengrocer's.
  d. There is a bus stop *in front of* the flower shop.
  e. There are two pubs. The Red Lion is in Station Road, *opposite* the flower shop *near* the railway bridge, and the Old Shepherd is *in* Church Street, *behind* the school.

3 Work in pairs.
Ask and answer questions about the picture.
Use the prepositions from exercise **2**.

> Where's the library?

> It's on the corner of Church Street and Lower Road, next to the post office and opposite the greengrocer's.

4 Here is a box of prepositions of movement.

| along | up | down | over | under |
| past | through | out of | in(to) | across |

This is the way you walk from Chesswood farm to the church. Put the correct preposition into the gaps.
You go _____ the path, _____ the pond, _____ the bridge, and _____ the gate. Then you go _____ the road and take the path _____ the wood. When you come _____ the wood you walk _____ the path and _____ the church. It takes five minutes.

5 [**T.19**] You will hear someone giving directions to get from school to her house. Listen and take notes. In pairs, compare your notes.
Give each other detailed directions to get to your house from your school, and take notes.

Now do the Stop and Check on page 36 of the Workbook.

UNIT 7

Fame

PRESENTATION

1 Read the text about Andrea de Silva.

● Grammar questions

– Underline the examples in the text of the Past Simple, and the time expressions that go with the Past Simple.
  started   at the age of fourteen
– All the other verb forms in the text are examples of the Present Perfect. Complete this rule:
  The Present Perfect is formed with the auxiliary verb _____ + the _____ _____.
– What is the difference between the following pairs of sentences?
  Why are different tenses used?

> She **has made** over twenty-five films.
> Charlie Chaplin **made** over fifty films.

> She **has travelled** to many parts of the world.
> She **went** to Argentina last year.

> She **has won** three Oscars.
> She **won** her first Oscar in 1987.

Andrea de Silva, the Hollywood actress, has made over 25 films in her career. She started acting at the age of fourteen. She has travelled to many parts of the world, including Australia, South America, and China.
I spoke to her last week and she said that her favourite place was Argentina. 'I went there a year ago when we made the western, *Good Times, Bad Times.*'
She has won three Oscars. She won her first Oscar in 1987 for her role as the scientist, Kay Brown, in *Texas Flower.*

2 Put the verbs in brackets in the correct tense, Present Perfect or Past Simple.

> Barbara Lively, the writer, is married with two children. She _____ (write) over 40 books. She _____ (start) writing after the death of her first husband. She _____ (live) in many parts of the world, including Japan and India.
> She _____ (spend) her childhood in Egypt, but _____ (come) to England in 1966.
> She _____ (write) both prose and poetry, but is best known for her romantic novels. She _____ (win) many awards, including the Booker Prize, which she _____ (win) in 1988 for the novel *Dark Times to Come*.

3 Now look back at the text about Andrea. Here are the answers to some questions about her.
Write in the questions.
a. How many _____?
Over 25.
b. When _____?
At the age of fourteen.
c. When _____?
A year ago.
d. _____?
Three.
e. _____?
In 1987.

Work in pairs.
Ask and answer similar questions about Barbara.

> **Rule**
> The Present Perfect expresses an action that happened some time before now.
> The Past Simple expresses an action that happened at a definite time in the past.

PRACTICE

1 Grammar

Write in the past tense forms and the past participles of the following verbs.
Some are regular, and some are irregular.

Infinitive	Past Tense	Past Participle
be	*was/were*	*been*
try		
act		
read		
have		
win		
break		
work		
write		
meet		
make		
sell		

2 Speaking and listening

1 Your teacher will give you a card which begins *Find someone who . . .*

> *Find someone who has been to Russia.*

You must form the question, beginning *Have you ever . . . ?*
Then stand up and ask everyone in the class.

2 Report back to the class.

> Two of us have been to Russia.
> None of us has been to Russia.
> Pierre is the only one who has been to Russia.

3 Ask questions to find out more about each other's experiences.

> When did you go to Russia?
> How long were you there?
> Where did you stay?
> Did you enjoy it?

3 Grammar

Make sentences and questions about the following people.

Example
Alice is a journalist.
- meet/a lot of famous people
  She has met a lot of famous people.
- interview/Prime Minister?
  Has she interviewed the Prime Minister?

a. Chris is a mountaineer.
   - climb/mountains all over the world
   - climb/Everest without oxygen
   - write/several books
   - ever have/an accident?

b. Paul Newman is an actor.
   - direct/many films
   - never win/an Oscar
   - ever write/a script?

c. Mike and Tina Walker are singers.
   - sell/over five million records
   - be/on tour all over the world
   - have/ten number one records
   - ever be/in a film?

PRESENTATION

1 | **T.20** | Read and listen to the following dialogues.

Tony	Where do you live, Ann?
Ann	In a house near Brighton.
Tony	How long have you lived there?
Ann	For three years.
Tony	Why did you move?
Ann	The house we had before was too small. We needed somewhere bigger.

Tony	What do you do, Ann?
Ann	I work in a bank.
Tony	How long have you worked there?
Ann	For eight years.
Tony	What did you do before that?
Ann	I worked for a travel agent.

● Grammar questions

- In each dialogue, Tony asks one question in the Present Simple, one in the Past Simple, and one in the Present Perfect. Which is which?
- Why are the different tenses used?
- Complete the following sentences about Ann.
  She _____ for three years.
  She _____ for eight years.
  She _____ because she needed somewhere bigger to live.
  She _____ before she joined the bank.

2 Complete the following similar dialogues between Tony and Ann.

Tony	Do you have a car, Ann?
Ann	Yes, I do.
Tony	How long _____ ?
Ann	For a year.
Tony	How much _____ pay for it?
Ann	About two thousand pounds.

Tony	_____ know a man called Lionel Beecroft?
Ann	Yes, _____ .
Tony	How long _____ ?
Ann	For years and years.
Tony	Where _____ ?
Ann	I met him while I was working for the travel agent.

> **Rule**
> The Present Perfect is also used to express an action or state which began in the past and continues to the present.

50

PRACTICE

1 Grammar

Work in pairs to decide which is the correct verb form.

a. *Have you ever seen/did you ever see* a rock concert?
b. *I saw/have seen* the Rolling Stones last year.
c. I love rock and roll. I *like/have liked* it all my life.
d. The Stones' concert *has been/was* excellent.
e. I *have bought/bought* all their records after the concert.
f. How long *have you known/do you know* Peter?
g. I *know him/have known* him since we were at school together.
h. When *did you get/have you got* married to him?
i. We *have been/are* together for over ten years, and we *have got/got* married eight years ago.

2 *For* or *since*?

For is used with a period of time. **Since** is used with a point in time (a day, a date, a time, an occasion).

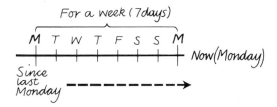

Put **for** or **since** into each gap.

a. _____ two weeks
b. _____ half an hour
c. _____ August
d. _____ 9.15
e. _____ I was ten
f. _____ a long time
g. _____ 3 March
h. _____ ages
i. _____ the beginning of term
j. _____ a couple of days

3 Speaking and listening

Work in pairs.
Ask and answer questions beginning *How long . . .?* about where you and your partner live, work, study, and about some of your possessions. Then try to get some more information.

> How long have you lived in . . .?
>
> How long have you worked . . .?
> What did you do before that?
>
> How long have you had your watch/jumper/car . . .?
> Where did you buy . . .?

● Language review

Present Perfect

The Present Perfect relates past actions and states to the present.

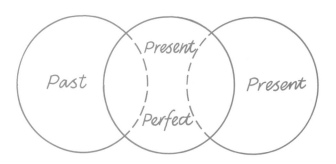

Here are two of its main uses:

1 It refers to an action in the past which is finished. *When* the action happened is not important. The action has some present importance.
   I've been to Scotland. (I know all about it.)
   Have you ever tried Indian food? (at any time in your life up to now)

2 It refers to an action or state which began in the past and continues to the present.
   I've had this book for three months. (I still have it.)
   How long have you worked here? (You still work here.)

Translate

I've been to the United States.

_____

I went there in 1987.

_____

Have you ever tried Indian food?

_____

I live in the capital city of my country.

_____

I've lived here all my life.

_____

Other uses of the Present Perfect are in Unit 14.

▶ **Grammar reference: page 126.**

SKILLS DEVELOPMENT

Reading

Pre-reading task
1 You are going to read an article about Paul Newman, the Hollywood film star. Look at the pictures. What do they tell you about Paul?
2 Work in groups. On a separate piece of paper, add to the charts.

What I know about Paul Newman	Questions I'd like to ask about Paul Newman
He's made a lot of films.	*Has he ever won an Oscar? How old is he?*

3 Compare your information and questions as a class.

Reading
Read the article, and try to find the answers to your questions.

Comprehension check
1 Which of your questions were answered?
2 What interested you most about Paul Newman? What did you learn that you didn't know before?
3 Here are summaries of the seven paragraphs of the article. Match them to the correct paragraph.

    a. ___ Some of his films.
    b. ___ His rise to stardom.
    c. ___ The end of one marriage, the beginning of another.
    d. ___ His early life.
    e. ___ The highs and lows of his later life.
    f. ___ His first professional work.
    g. ___ Newman the person, not the movie star.

4 Here are the answers to some questions from paragraphs 1–3. What are the questions?
    a. In 1925.
    b. After graduating.
    c. While they were acting together.
    d. In 1949.
    e. Three.
    f. He was thirty.
    g. A Greek slave.
    h. No, he didn't (enjoy making the film).
    i. About Graziano's childhood.
Write some questions based on paragraphs 4–7. Ask the rest of the class your questions.

Vocabulary
1 There are two other words that mean a *film* in the text. Find them. Which one is mainly American English?

Paul Newman
actor, director, racing driver

Paul Newman, actor, director, and racing driver, was born so good-looking that people said it was a shame to waste such beauty on a boy. He was born in Cleveland, Ohio, in 1925, and did some acting in high school and college, but never seriously considered making it his future career. However, after graduating, he immediately started working in the theatre. He met his first wife, Jackie Witte, while they were acting together, and they got married in 1949. They had three children, a boy and two girls.

2 He found work in the theatre and on several TV shows in New York. When he was thirty, he went to Los Angeles and made his first film. It was what Newman called an 'uncomfortable' start in the movies, in the role of a Greek slave. The experience was so bad that he went back to the theatre, and didn't accept another film role for two years.

3 The film he chose was his big break. He played the boxer, Rocky Graziano, in the film *Someone up There Likes Me*. Newman is a method actor who believes in living the part before beginning the film. He spent days – from morning till night – with Graziano. He studied the fighter's speech and watched him box, and they talked endlessly about Graziano's childhood. The picture brought Newman stardom overnight.

4 He was living in Los Angeles away from his family when he met Joanne Woodward, an actress who he had first met in New York. They worked together in *The Long Hot Summer*. His wife, Jackie, and Paul recognized that their marriage wasn't working, and got divorced. Newman and Miss Woodward were married in Las Vegas in 1958.

5 Newman went on to make films such as *Cat on a Hot Tin Roof*, *The Hustler*, *Butch Cassidy and the Sundance Kid*, *The Sting* and *Towering Inferno*. He has made over forty-five films, and has won many awards, but he has never won an Oscar.

6 His marriage to Woodward is one of the longest and strongest in Hollywood. They have three daughters, and they have co-starred in six films. Ever since the film *Winning*, Newman has been passionately interested in car racing, and in 1979 he came second in the twenty-four hour Le Mans race. But the end of the 1970s was not all good news for him. In 1978 his only son, Scott, died of a drug overdose, and as a result Newman created the Scott Newman Foundation to inform young people on drug abuse.

7 He has a strong social conscience, and has supported causes such as the anti-nuclear movement, the environment, and driver education. All the money from 'Newman's Own' salad dressing, popcorn, and spaghetti sauce, now a multi-million dollar business, goes to charity. He is more than just a movie star. 'I would like to be remembered as a man who has tried to help people to communicate with each other,' says Newman, 'and who has tried to do something good with his life. You have to keep trying. That's the most important thing.'

2 Match a word in the text to the following definitions.
Paragraph 1
  a. to use badly or unproductively (e.g. *time/money*)
  b. a profession or occupation
Paragraph 2
  c. a person who is the 'property' of someone else and who has to work for them
Paragraph 3
  d. a lucky opportunity that leads to success
  e. the state of being a star
Paragraph 6
  f. more of something (e.g. *a drug*) than is safe
  g. using something in the wrong way
Paragraph 7
  h. a person's understanding of what is right and wrong
  i. an organization that helps people who need help
  j. to do something again and again

Writing
Write about a living film star, or a musician (or group) that you admire. Write about their background, their successes, and why you like them.

Do the exercise on page 41 of the Workbook first.

● **Vocabulary**

Homophones

There are many words in English with the same pronunciation but a different spelling and meaning.

Example
/hɪə/   here – *Come here!*
         hear – *I can't hear you!*

1 For each of the following words, find a word in the text about Paul Newman with the same pronunciation but a different spelling.

waist	_____	knew	_____
roll	_____	our	_____
too	_____	sun	_____
brake	_____		

2 Think of the homophone for these words.

there	_____	ate	_____
red	_____	sea	_____
been	_____	check	_____
sail	_____	fair	_____
by	_____	week	_____
I	_____	right	_____

3 Write the words in exercises 1 and 2 on the correct line according to the vowel sound.
  a. /ʌ/ _____   f. /eə/ _____
  b. /eɪ/ _____   g. /aɪ/ _____
  c. /uː/ *two*   h. /aʊə/ _____
  d. /iː/ _____   i. /əʊ/ _____
  e. /e/ _____

53

Adverbs

1 Many adverbs end in **-ly**.
   slowly   carefully   fortunately
   Find three examples of adverbs that end in **-ly** in the text about Paul Newman.

2 There are also many adverbs that don't end in **-ly**!
   too   even   together
   Put one of the adverbs in the box into each gap. Sometimes more than one adverb is possible.

of course	at last	especially	still
even	exactly	at least	nearly
always	too	fortunately	only

a. I saw a car crash today. _____ , nobody was hurt.
b. I called at Pat and Fred's house at ten o'clock this morning, but they were _____ in bed.
c. I like all Russian writers, _____ Tolstoy.
d. I got up late this morning. I _____ missed the bus, but I ran and caught it.
e. His house has got everything – _____ a swimming pool.
f. 'I hate ironing.'
   'Me _____ .'
g. You've arrived at _____ the right moment. Your lunch is on the table.
h. 'How much does she earn?'
   'She's the director, so I'm sure she gets fifty thousand a year, _____ .'
i. I will _____ love you.
j. 'Do you study hard?'
   '_____ I do. I want to pass my exams.'
k. He walked out of the prison. _____ , after fifteen years, he was a free man.
l. My son is very difficult to feed. He eats _____ fruit and crisps.

● Listening and speaking

Interview with a musician

Pre-listening task
1 Work in groups. How many musical instruments do you know the names of?
2 Read the definitions of some of the words in the interview.

   keyboards (*n*) piano, organ, and synthesizer
   a band (*n*) another word for a group of musicians
   a hit record (*n*) a successful record
   to tour (*v*) to visit lots of places in a country or round the world
   an album (*n*) a long-playing record

Listening

T.21   You will hear an interview with Paul Carrack, the lead vocalist with a band called Mike and the Mechanics. As you listen, put a tick (√) or a cross (×) on the chart.

Instruments he plays	Bands he has played with	Places he has visited
guitar	Roxy Music	France
saxophone	U2	Japan
trumpet	The Smiths	America
drums	The Pretenders	Eastern Europe
keyboards	Simply Red	Germany
violin	Madness	Italy
piano	Queen	South America
	Ace	

Which bands has he played with?
What countries has he been to?

Comprehension check

1 How many jobs has Paul had?
2 Did he have music lessons?
3 Was he already making money as a musician when he left school?
4 What was special about the song *How long?*
5 Did he want to go to America?
6 Why do his records do well in America?
7 He has had a busy year. What has he done?
8 Make sentences about Paul with the numbers and phrases in boxes **A** and **B**.

   Example
   twenty years – *He has been in the music business for about twenty years.*

A	B
five years old	since 1985
sixteen years old	about twenty
1974	

Language work

1 What tense are the verb forms you used for box **A** on page 54? What about the verb forms in **B**?

2 Correct the mistakes in verb forms in the following sentences.
   a. Paul is a professional musician for twenty years.
   b. He has started playing the drums when he was five.
   c. He played with Mike and the Mechanics for several years.
   d. He never went to South America.
   e. He has had a hit with a song called *How long?* in 1974.
   f. He is interested in music all his life.

Roleplay

Some of you are members of a group of musicians (classical, pop, jazz).
Some of you are journalists who are going to interview the musicians.

Musicians
Work in groups of three or four.
Talk together to decide the following:
– the kind of music you play
– the name of your band/orchestra
– who plays what
– what has influenced your music
– how long you have been together
– the records you have made
– the countries you have toured.

Journalists
There needs to be one journalist for every group of musicians. Work together to think of some questions to ask the musicians. When you are ready, conduct the interview.

● Everyday English

Short answers

1 Notice how, in answers to **yes/no** questions, we often repeat the subject and the auxiliary verb. We don't just say **Yes** or **No**.

*'**Do you** like cooking?'*	*'Yes, **I do**.'*
*'**Is it** raining?'*	*'No, **it isn't**.'*
*'**Have you** got a car?'*	*'Yes, **I have**.'*
*'**Are you** good at chess?'*	*'No, **I'm not**.'*

2 Work alone. Think of two questions to ask a partner. Use the prompts.
   a. Do you like (football) . . .?
   b. Can you (type/ride a horse) . . .?
   c. Did you (go out/do any work) . . . last night?
   d. Have you ever (go skiing/dream in English) . . .?
   e. Have you got (a cat/a car) . . .?
   f. Are you good at (cooking/golf) . . .?

3 Work in pairs. Ask your questions, and reply to your partner's questions using short answers.

UNIT 8

Pros and cons

PRESENTATION

1 | **T.22a** | Kathy has left her job as a shop assistant because she wants to open a restaurant. Listen to her conversation with a friend, and fill in the chart.

Advantages of having a restaurant	Disadvantages of having a restaurant

2 | **T.22b** | Listen to the pronunciation of **have to** (/hæf tʊ/or/tə/).

3 In pairs, practise saying the sentences from the conversation with **have to** and **don't have to**.

● Grammar questions

– What is the difference between the uses of **have** in the following sentences?
*I **have** a new car.*
*I **have** to work hard.*
– What is the difference in pronunciation between the two uses?

PRACTICE

1 Grammar

Make as many sentences as possible from the chart.

Politicians Postmen/women Teachers Nurses Air hostesses Factory workers	have to don't have to	work in shifts. do some/any work at home. wear a uniform. make speeches. get up early.

2 Listening and speaking

1 Work in pairs.
Choose one of the jobs from the pictures opposite, or a job from exercise **1** above. Don't say what it is! Your partner will ask questions to find out what it is.

> Do you have to work outside/ use your hands/be fit/ be good at ...?

> Yes, I do./No, I don't.

56

2 Which of the jobs above *wouldn't* you like to do? Say why not.

> I wouldn't like to be a nurse. Nurses have to work very long hours, and don't earn much.

3 Grammar

The past of **have to** is **had to** (/hæt tʊ/or/tə/).
Why didn't Kathy like her job as a shop assistant?

> She didn't like it because she had to wear a uniform.

57

PRESENTATION

The Indy is a newspaper for the 'young and independent', and it has a problem page.
Match a heading to a letter and to an answer from Daisy.
Do you agree with the advice?

PROBLEM PAGE

ASK DAISY

If you have a problem that you want to get off your chest, write to Daisy at:
The Indy
40 City Road
London EC1Y 2DB

Never been kissed

Food for thought

To dye, or not to dye?

I LIVE on a farm, and I have started thinking about animal rights. Now I am a vegetarian. My problem is that my parents are furious. My Mum doesn't cook anything different for me, so every night all I eat is vegetables and bread and cheese. I don't think this is fair. Why can't she cook me something tasty?
Michelle, 17

MY PARENTS went away on holiday recently, so I decided to dye my hair. I am blonde and I dyed my hair black. Now it looks awful and I don't know what to do.

A couple of days ago my parents came home, and when my Mum saw my hair, she went completely mad. Now, as a punishment, she says I can't dye it back. What should I do?
Lucy, 16

I'M 16 and I have never been out with a girl. I've never even kissed one. My friends have all had lots of girlfriends, but girls don't seem to be interested in me. Now I tell everyone that I have a girlfriend in France, but I don't think they believe me. What should I do?
Richard, 16

I think you should dye your hair back to its original colour. Tell your mother first that this is what you're going to do if you want to, but I'm sure she'll be pleased to see her 'old' daughter again.

People of your age, especially boys, often tell stories about their experiences. I'm sure some of your friends are telling stories too! You shouldn't tell lies, because that will make you feel more worried, and people will learn the truth sooner or later.
Don't worry about not having a girlfriend. Your time will come.

I think you're being a little selfish. *You* chose to stop eating meat, not your parents. Your mother is probably a very busy woman. I think you should cook for yourself. Baked potatoes are very easy!

● Grammar questions

– What verb is used to ask for or give a suggestion?
– *She has to cook for herself.*
  She should cook for herself.
  Which sentence expresses an obligation?

PRACTICE

1 Speaking and writing

1 Work in pairs.
Look at some other letters written to Daisy's problem page. What should the people do?

NOT FAIR
I get £1.50 a week pocket money, but most of my friends get much more. When I ask my Mum and Dad for more, they say I can have more if I help in the house, but I don't see why I should. Mum's at home all day, and it's *her* job to look after the house, not mine. What do you think?
Sharon, 14

WEIGHTY PROBLEM
Girls don't find me attractive, and I think the reason is that I'm fat. Ever since I was about seven, I've been on the chubby side, but it didn't worry me until now. I'm quite intelligent and have lots of friends but not the type I'd like. What should I do?
Peter, 14

BULLIES AT SCHOOL
Please help me, because I'm in terrible trouble. There are bullies at my school who hit me and kick me, and they say I have to give them money or they will really hurt me. I'm frightened of them. I haven't got any money to give them. Please tell me what to do.
Jeremy, 14

ROSES ARE RED . . .
I am in love with a girl who is very attractive. A friend introduced us. She doesn't know how I feel. I have her address and telephone number, but I don't know what to do. Should I call her? I could send her some roses or chocolates, but I can't decide which is better. If I send something, what should I write on the card?
Andrew, 15

PROBLEMS WITH LESSONS
I'm very worried because the lessons at school are too difficult for me. I don't understand them, but the others in the class know what the teachers are talking about. Who should I talk to? We have exams soon, and I know I'm going to fail them. My parents will be furious, because they think I'm doing OK. Please help.
Suzie, 17

MY FRIENDS STEAL
Some of my friends steal things from shops after school. Usually it's sweets, but some of them steal bigger things too, and sell them or just give them away. They keep telling me to go with them, and call me names because I don't want to. They say I'm a coward. I don't want to steal, but I don't want to look stupid, either. What should I do?
Simon, 13

2 Choose one of the letters, and, with a partner, write a letter in reply. Try to express sympathy with the problem and give some explanation as well as practical advice.

2 Speaking and listening

You are talking to someone who is coming to stay in your country for six months. What advice can you give? Use **should**, **have to**, and **don't have to**.

> You should learn the language.
> You have to have a passport.
> You don't have to get a visa.

Include advice about the following:

| money | documents | clothes |
| health | accommodation | |

● Language review

Expressing obligation

Have to expresses strong obligation.
Don't have to expresses absence of obligation.
Should expresses mild obligation or advice.

> **Translate**
>
> Nurses have to work long hours.
>
> _____
>
> I don't have to get up early at the weekend.
>
> _____
>
> You should see a doctor.
>
> _____

▶ Grammar reference: page 126.

SKILLS DEVELOPMENT

● Reading

You will read about two special teenagers.

Reading and vocabulary

1 Read the text about David Bolton quite quickly. Find four words (not more) that you don't know, and check them in your dictionary.
2 Compare with a partner the four words you each looked up.

David the teenage tycoon

1 TEENAGER DAVID BOLTON has just put £9,000 in the bank – after only six months of part-time work as a computer consultant. The electronics expert from Croydon, South London, is fast establishing a reputation as one of the country's top troubleshooters – the person to call if no one else can cope.

2 For David, 15, his first steps to fame and fortune began when he was only nine, when his parents bought him a computer, a ZX-90. 'I soon learned to program it. I needed something bigger, so I had to save for ages to buy an Amstrad.'

3 It was only about a year ago, however, that he decided to get serious about computing. He went to night school to learn how to write business programs, and did a correspondence course with an American college.

4 He got in touch with a computer seller, Eltec, who were so impressed they gave him computers and software worth more than £3,000. In return, he has to send them a monthly report saying what he has done and what his plans are. He helps companies by suggesting which computers they should buy, and by writing individual programs for them.

5 He can work more quickly than many older professionals. In one case, he went to a company where a professional programmer worked for six months and couldn't find the problem. David finished the job in five days.

Reading for information

Now read the text more carefully and answer the questions.

Comprehension check

1 What is special about David?
2 How did he become interested in computers?
3 Was it easy to learn? What did he have to do?
4 What does he have to do in his job?
5 Why is he successful?
6 What advice does he give to others?
7 Here are the answers to some questions. Work out the questions.
   a. Nine thousand pounds.
   b. A ZX-90.
   c. Because he wanted to buy an Amstrad computer.
   d. By suggesting which computers they should buy, and by writing programs for them.
   e. More equipment.

6 It is because of work of this standard that in the short period he has been in business David has made about £9,000. With it he has bought more equipment.

7 How did he do it? 'You have to be ambitious, and you have to really want to get to the top. Believe in yourself, and tell yourself that you're the best.'

Arranging a jumbled text

The seven paragraphs in the text about David are organized as follows:

1 – an interesting introduction
2 – some background
3 – training
4 – details about the work
5 – one particular job
6 – what he has done with his money
7 – advice to others

Now read the seven jumbled paragraphs about Kimora Lee Perkins, and put them in the right order. The order should be the same as in the text about David.

1 _____ 2 _____ 3 _____ 4 _____ 5 _____ 6 _____ 7 _____

Mademoiselle Chanel

a. She owes her remarkable looks to a Korean mother and a black father. But when she was young, back home in St. Louis, Missouri, she cried when she looked in the mirror and saw how tall she was. 'I felt I was different from all the other kids my age,' she explains. Her mother Joanne Perkins, 34, recalls, 'Kimora was a tormented child. It was almost impossible for her to relate to other girls of her age, and there was a lot of teasing. Growing up was a very painful experience for her.'

b. She is not only the youngest top model, she is also one of the richest. 'Mom looks after that,' Kimora explains, 'I don't even have a credit card – I'm too young!'

c. When she was 11, her mother took her to a local modelling school. She thought modelling would be an interesting job because then she would be with other tall girls. She began to like it very much, and had to learn how to walk and pose to show off the clothes to their best advantage.

d. 'People think it's a very easy job that anyone could do, but you need a lot of stamina,' Kimora says. 'Once, in London, we had to take photos in the street all through the night, and then I had to go to my tutor for school lessons at 9.00 am before taking the daytime photos at 1.00pm.'

e. SHE'S 14, American, and speaks no French at all. But six-foot-tall Kimora Lee Perkins is hot news in Paris. She has become the top model at the Parisian fashion house of Chanel.

f. What advice does she have for others? 'You should go to a good modelling school, and you have to be prepared to work really hard and give your whole life to modelling.'

g. Chanel chose her because 'she has the look of the 90s', and now she spends eight to ten hours a day modelling their latest fashions in various parts of the world. 'I have to try really hard to keep looking good for the cameras,' she said.

Comprehension check

Work in pairs.

1 Ask and answer the same comprehension check questions as for David.

> What is special about Kimora?
> How did she become interested in modelling?

2 Write some questions about Kimora to ask the other members of the class.

> Does she speak French?

● Discussion

Work in groups of four or five to discuss the questions. If you still live at home, answer in the present tense. If you have left home, answer in the past tense.

1 What $\begin{vmatrix} do \\ did \end{vmatrix}$ you have to do to help in the house? What about your brothers and sisters?

'Mum and Dad are parents, not people!'

'Is that you, Mother? Can you make me some coffee?'

2 $\begin{vmatrix} Can \\ Could \end{vmatrix}$ you stay out as long as you $\begin{vmatrix} want, \\ wanted, \end{vmatrix}$

or $\begin{vmatrix} do \\ did \end{vmatrix}$ you have to be home by a certain time?

3 $\begin{vmatrix} Can \\ Could \end{vmatrix}$ you go where you $\begin{vmatrix} want \\ wanted \end{vmatrix}$ (discos, parties)?

4 $\begin{vmatrix} Do \\ Did \end{vmatrix}$ you have to tell your parents where

you $\begin{vmatrix} are \\ were \end{vmatrix}$ going?

5 $\begin{vmatrix} Do \\ Did \end{vmatrix}$ you argue about money, clothes, friends, school work, or anything else?

● Vocabulary

Nouns that go together

1 In English, many nouns can go together to make a new word.

*post + office = **post office***
*head + ache = **headache***
*horse + race = **horse-race***

Sometimes they are written as one word, sometimes two, and sometimes they are written with a hyphen (-). The stress is usually on the first word.

'post office ‎ 'headache ‎ 'horse-race

Match a line in **A** with a line in **B**. Check the spelling in your dictionary.
(The stress is on the first word in all the combinations.)

A	B		A	B
alarm	opener		hair	board
car	recorder		fire	case
traffic	table		sun	drier
tooth	coat		screw	post
cigarette	lights		word	ring
tin	paste		ear	bin
tape	park		dust	engine
earth	lounge		sign	set
departure	money		book	hour
pocket	clock		notice	belt
time	lighter		rush	driver
rain	quake		safety	processor

2 Make sentences, using one of the words above. Say where you see it or what you do with it. The others must guess what it is.

> You wear it in the rain.

> A raincoat.

3 There are about ten noun + noun combinations in the texts on pages 60 and 61. Try to find them!

Example
credit card

Make or *do*?

These two words have similar meanings, and it can be difficult to know which one to use.
Do is usually the correct word when we are talking about work.
Make often expresses the idea of creation or construction. But there are exceptions to these rules!

1 Put **make** or **do** before the following nouns.

_____ a phone call ‎ ‎ ‎ _____ my homework
_____ a mess ‎ ‎ ‎ _____ my bed (in the morning)
_____ the washing-up ‎ ‎ ‎ _____ someone a favour
_____ the ironing ‎ ‎ ‎ _____ the shopping
_____ a cup of tea ‎ ‎ ‎ _____ a mistake
_____ your best ‎ ‎ ‎ _____ a noise

2 Work in pairs. Write short conversations to practise some of the **make**/**do** + noun combinations.

> Do you have to make your bed in the morning?

> Yes, I do.

> Was your homework good?

> I made a lot of mistakes. I have to do it again.

Listening

Holidays in January

Pre-listening task

Discuss the following questions in groups.

1 Where do people in your country like to go for their summer holidays? Do they often go abroad or do they visit other parts of their own country?
2 Do many people go for winter holidays? Where would you like to go for a winter holiday? Somewhere hot or somewhere cold?

Listening and note-taking

T.23 You will hear three people giving advice about visiting their country in the month of January. Listen and make notes in the chart. Your teacher will stop the tape after each section for you to check your notes with a partner.

5 Look at the pictures. Which holidays do they go with?

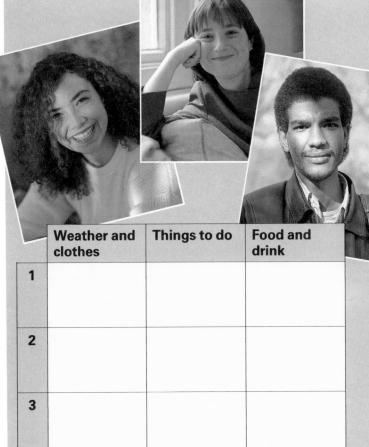

	Weather and clothes	Things to do	Food and drink
1			
2			
3			

Comprehension check

1 Can you guess which countries they are talking about? What helped you?
2 Which two people talk about sports? Which sports?
3 Which two people talk about money? What do they say?
4 Which holiday do you think is the most cultural? Why?

6 Which of the three places would you most like to visit in January? Why?

Language work/speaking

1 Put the following words in the right order to ask about holidays.

a. weather/is/like/in/what/the/January?

_____

b. take/clothes/what/I/should?

_____

c. can/things/sort/of/what/do/I?

_____

d. cash/cheques/I/should/or/travellers'/take?

_____

e. food/you/recommend/do/what?

_____

f. special/any/there/places/are/should/go/to/I?

_____

2 If possible, work with a student who comes from a different country. What advice can you give about visiting *your* country in the month of January?

2 Listen again, and practise the dialogues in pairs.
3 Notice the following:

Inviting	*Would you like to . . . ?*
Refusing	*I can't, I'm afraid.*
	I have to . . .
	I'm going . . .
	That's very kind, but . . .
Accepting	*Yes, I'd love to!*
	That would be lovely!

4 Work in pairs.
Practise dialogues of inviting, accepting, and refusing. Use the following ideas, or your own if you want.

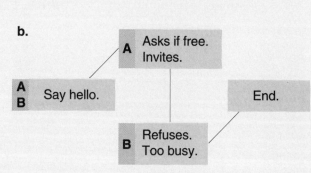

go to the theatre   go for a coffee

go for a walk   come to a party   play tennis

come round (to my house) for a meal

● **Everyday English**

Invitations

1 **T.24** Listen to three dialogues inviting friends out. Which follows which pattern below?

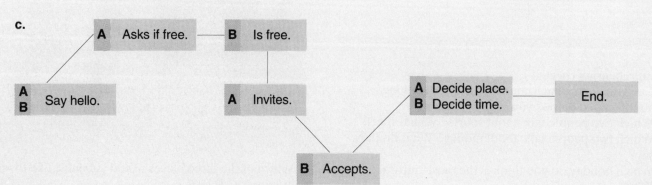

a.
- A: Asks if free. Invites.
- A B: Say hello.
- B: Refuses. Already has plans to go out.
- End.

b.
- A: Asks if free. Invites.
- A B: Say hello.
- B: Refuses. Too busy.
- End.

c.
- A: Asks if free.
- B: Is free.
- A B: Say hello.
- A: Invites.
- B: Accepts.
- A: Decide place. B: Decide time.
- End.

UNIT 9

Will – First Conditional – Time clauses – Travelling

Life in the 21st century

PRESENTATION

Where will people live in the twenty-first century?
1 Read the text about Japan.

Living in the skies

Louise Hidalgo considers life in the 21st century, with two-kilometre high buildings, and Japanese cities that touch the sky.

Imagine a building one third of the height of Mount Everest, built by robots, and containing a whole city. Imagine you can walk out of your front door in a T-shirt and shorts on a cold winter's day and take a lift down 500
5 floors to school. Imagine you can see the sea a mile below you. Imagine you can never open a window. Imagine . . .

Well, if Japanese architects find enough money for their project, in the 21st century you'll be able to live in a
10 building like that.

Ohbayashi Gumi has designed a two-kilometre high building, Aeropolis, which will stand right in the middle of Tokyo Bay. Over 300,000 people will live in it. It will be 500 floors high, and in special lifts it will take just 15
15 minutes to get from top to bottom. Restaurants, offices, flats, cinemas, schools, hospitals, and post offices will all be just a few lift stops away. According to the architects, Aeropolis will be the first 'city to touch the skies'.

'When we get to the end of this century, Tokyo will have
20 a population of over 15 million people,' said design manager Mr Shuzimo. 'There isn't enough land in Japan. We're going to start doing tests to find the best place to build it. I hope people will like living on the 500th floor.'

Going up and up. It will take twenty-five years to build Aeropolis and it will cost over £2,000 million.

Won't people want to have trees and flowers around
25 them? 'We're going to have green floors, where children can play and office workers can eat their lunch-break sandwiches,' explained Mr Shuzimo. What about fires? 'If there is a fire, it will be put out by robots. I hope we'll get the money we need to build. As soon as we do, we'll
30 start. This will be the most exciting building in the world.'

2 Ask and answer questions about Aeropolis, using the following numbers.

Example
twenty-five

How long will it take to build Aeropolis?

Twenty-five years.

- two thousand million
- two (kilometres)
- five hundred
- three hundred thousand
- fifteen
- fifteen million

3 Would you like to live in Aeropolis? Why/why not?

4 Mr Shuzimo expresses two future intentions (with **going to**) and two hopes.
Find them in the text.

● Grammar questions

- *It will take twenty-five years to build Aeropolis.*
  It will cost over £2,000,000,000.
  Do these sentences express future intentions or future facts?
- ***When*** *we get to the end of this century, Tokyo will have a population of over fifteen million people.*
  If *there is a fire, it will be put out by robots.*
  Which sentence expresses something that is sure to happen? Which is just a possibility?
- When will they start to build Aeropolis?

PRACTICE

1 Speaking

1 Look at what Jenny and Mark hope will happen in the future. Make sentences using **If . . . , . . . will . . .**

Examples
*If I **don't go** out so much, I'**ll do** more work.*
*If I **do** more work, I'**ll** . . .*

Jenny
↓
If . . . I don't go out so much
↓
do more work
↓
pass my exams
↓
go to university
↓
study medicine
↓
become a doctor
↓
earn a good salary
↓
?

Mark
↓
If . . . I stop smoking
↓
have more money
↓
save some every week
↓
rich when I'm thirty
↓
have my own business
↓
make a lot of money
↓
retire when I'm forty
↓
?

2 | T.25 | Listen to the sentences and repeat them.

3 Ask and answer questions about Jenny and Mark.

What will Jenny do if she passes her exams?

She'll go to university.

2 Speaking and listening

Work in pairs.
One of you is going skiing for the first time.
The other sees all the problems! Use the prompts below.

What will you do if there's no snow?

We'll go walking!

- don't like the food?
- it rains?
- don't learn to ski?
- hurt yourself?
- lose your money?
- you don't understand the language?
- you don't know anyone?
- there's nowhere to go in the evening?

3 Grammar

1 Put **when** or **if** into each gap.
  a. _____ I go home tonight, I'll have a bath.
  b. _____ there is a good programme on TV, I'll watch it.
  c. _____ there's nothing in the fridge, we'll eat out.
  d. I'll pay you back the money _____ I get my next pay cheque.
  e. We'll go skiing next winter _____ we have enough money.
  f. _____ it's a nice day tomorrow, we'll go swimming.
  g. I'm coming to London tomorrow. I'll phone you _____ I arrive.
  h. We're thinking of going to Spain for our holidays. _____ we decide to go, I'll let you know.

2

If When As soon as	I see Peter, I'll tell him the news.

Notice the use of the Present Simple (not **will**) in the first clause. Put **if**, **when**, or **as soon as** into each box, and put the verbs in brackets in the correct tense.

Paul Bye, darling. Have a good trip.

Mary Thanks. I _____ (ring) you _____ I _____ (arrive) at the hotel.

Paul That's lovely, but remember I'm going out.

Mary Well, _____ you _____ (be) out _____ I _____ (ring), I _____ (leave) a message on the answer phone so you know I've arrived safely.

Paul Great. What time do you expect you'll be there?

Mary _____ the plane _____ (arrive) on time, I _____ (be) at the hotel at about 10.00. That's 8.00 your time.

Paul All right. And remember. Give me a ring _____ you know the time of your flight back, and I _____ (pick) you up.

Mary Thanks, darling. Bye!

Language review

Will

In Unit 5, we saw that **will** can express a future intention made at the moment of speaking. In this unit, we see that **will** can also express a future fact.

> **Translate**
>
> Thousands of people will live in Aeropolis.
>
> _____
>
> It won't be ready until 2015.
>
> _____

First Conditional

The First Conditional expresses a possible situation and its result.

If it rains at the weekend	→	I'll stay at home.

= the condition = possible and real	→	the result

> **Translate**
>
> If it rains, I'll stay at home.
>
> _____
>
> What will you do if you have no more money?
>
> _____
>
> If you're late, I won't wait for you.
>
> _____

Time clauses with *when* and *as soon as*

In the time clause, we use a present tense to talk about the future.

> **Translate**
>
> I'll tell him the news when I see him.
>
> _____
>
> As soon as I arrive, I'll ring you.
>
> _____

▶ **Grammar reference: page 127.**

SKILLS DEVELOPMENT

● Listening

How 'green' are you?

Pre-listening task

1 We are much more aware now of the need to look after our environment.
   Make two lists of things we *should* do and things we *shouldn't* do if we want to protect the planet.
2 What stories about the environment are in the news at the moment?

Listening for information

You will hear an interview with John Baines, an educational consultant who writes books about the environment. He talks about how he tries to be 'green', that is, to be friendly to the environment.

T.26 Listen and put a tick (✓) next to the things in the pictures that he talks about.

Comprehension check

1 What are some of the things he talks about that are *not* in the pictures?
2 What are some of the things he does *more* of and some of the things he does *less* of?
3 Complete the following sentences.
   a. John uses his bicycle more because _____.
   b. He's going to try to use less petrol by _____.
   c. He uses unleaded petrol because _____.
   d. When the bags in his kitchen are full, _____.
   e. He's a vegetarian because _____.
   f. John thinks that if we don't look after _____.

What do you think?

1 How 'green' are you? What have you done to be more friendly to the environment?
2 John thinks that people should try to change their lifestyle little by little, not all at once.
   How could *you* become more 'green'?

> I could walk more.

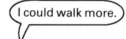

● Reading and speaking

Pre-reading task

Work in three groups.

1 Discuss the advantages and disadvantages of one of the following forms of transport.

   cars   trains   bicycles

> Cars take you door to door.
> Cars can be difficult to park.

2 Think of some current TV advertisements for cars. What are they saying about the car and its driver?

68

THE ROAD TO RUIN

The M25, the motorway around London, opened in 1986. Today people call it the biggest car park in Europe. Every morning on the radio we hear about jams, and road repairs, and (a)_____, and which parts of the M25 to avoid. One day soon we will hear 'There is a traffic jam all the (b)_____ round the M25 in both directions. If you are driving to work, we advise you to go back home.'

Winston Churchill described the car as the curse of the twentieth (c)_____. This will probably be true of the next century, (d)__. It can be very funny to compare advertisements for cars with the reality of driving them. Cars are symbols of freedom, wealth, and masculinity. But when you are (e)_____ in a traffic jam, all cars are just little metal boxes to sit in.

> 5,000 people a year are killed on British roads, and 40,000 are injured. For children, road accidents are a major cause of death.

Cities and towns all over the world have a (f)_____ problem, and no government really knows what to do. For once it is not a matter of technology which is stopping us. If we want to build two-level roads, we can do it. If we want trains which can travel at hundreds of miles an hour, we can build them.

The problem is a question of principle. Should we look to road or rail for our transport needs? Should the Government, or private companies, control them? And either way, who should pay?

The people who believe in roads say that cars represent a personal (g)_____ to travel when and where you want to. But on trains and buses – public transport – you have to travel when the (h)_____ says you can. These people think that if you build more roads, the traffic will move more quickly, but research shows that if there are more roads, there will be more cars to fill them.

By 2010, the number of cars on our roads will double. Environmentalists are saying that we should put more money into public transport. Cars often carry just one (i)_____. If the public transport system works, more people will use it. If trains carry more people, the roads won't be so crowded, and cars pollute the air more than trains.

> By 2025, just to park all the cars in Britain will need an area larger than London.

One characteristic of the people of the twentieth century is that we are a (j)_____ on the move. But it is just possible that soon we won't be able to move another inch, and we'll have to stay exactly where we are!

Reading and gap-filling
Read the text and fill each gap with one of these words.

choice	stuck	century	crashes	huge	
person	way	timetable	too	race	

Comprehension check
1 Say if the following sentences are true or false.
   a. You can park your car on the M25.
   b. There is often a jam all the way round the M25.
   c. Winston Churchill thought cars were an awful invention.
   d. Advertisements for cars don't show the reality of driving.
   e. We do not have the technology to find a solution to the traffic problem.
   f. We need to decide what our principles are if we want to solve the traffic problem.
   g. Some people think that the traffic will move more quickly if there are more roads.
   h. Environmentalists think that public transport should be more expensive.
2 Did the article mention any of the advantages and disadvantages of cars and trains that you discussed?
3 What are the reasons for building more roads?
4 What are the reasons for improving the public transport system?

What do you think?
1 What is the traffic situation like in your town? Is there a good public transport system?
Is it cheap? Do you have to pay to use the motorways? Do people drive well?
2 Tell each other about a time you were stuck in a traffic jam.

Speaking
Work in groups of five to do *one* of the following.
Either
Prepare and act out a roleplay using the five roles below. You are discussing how best to solve the traffic situation in your town.
Role A You want to build more roads. (Where? Who will pay?)
Role B You want to improve the public transport system. (How? Will it have to make a profit?)
Role C You are a cyclist.
Role D You often walk around town, going to work or doing the shopping.
Role E You are a shopkeeper.
Or
Work together to devise a transport survey. Think of questions to ask people about their travel habits.

Examples
How many cars does your family have?
How often are they used?
Does your family use the car for short journeys?

Try to get as much information as possible.

How many ways can you travel to school?
How often do you use public transport?

You could type the survey, and ask students from other classes to answer the questions!

● Vocabulary

1 Travelling by rail

The words in the box are all to do with travelling by train. Look them up in your dictionary to check the meaning and the pronunciation, then fill in the diagram.

> ticket office   buffet car   show (your ticket)
> get on   café   single   ticket inspector
> passenger   get off   miss   driver
> information office   compartment   season
> platform   waiting room   catch   return

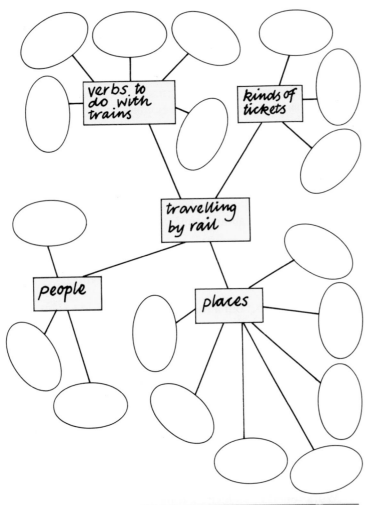

2 Travelling by air

1 Work in pairs.
Make a similar diagram about travelling by air. You decide what groups to have.

2 The following sentences describe what you do when you go to an airport to catch a plane, but they are in the wrong order.
Read them carefully and put them in the right order.

_____ You go to the departure lounge.
_____ You get a trolley.
_____ You arrive at the airport.
_____ You go to your gate.
_____ You go to the check-in desk.
_____ You go to the duty-free shop.
_____ You get a boarding card.
_____ You board the plane.
_____ You check in your luggage.
_____ You look at the departure board to see if your flight is boarding yet.
_____ The board tells you which gate to go to.
_____ You go through passport control.

3 What is the order of events when you fly into an airport? Begin like this:

The plane lands.
You unfasten your seat-belt.

● Everyday English

Travelling

1 **T.27a** You will hear some lines of dialogue. Say if the dialogues are taking place at an airline check-in desk or at a railway ticket office.

2 **T.27b** Listen to the complete dialogue at the check-in desk. With a partner, try to remember the dialogue.

3 **T.27c** Listen to the complete dialogue at the ticket office. Practise the questions.

4 Work in pairs. You are going to practise dialogues at a ticket office. Imagine it is 11.00 am.

Student A Look at the information on page 119.
Student B You want to go to Bristol. Ask for information about train times and ticket prices. Decide what kind of ticket you want and how you are going to pay.

Begin like this:
Student A *Good morning. Can I help you?*
Student B *Yes, please. I . . .*

5 Now change roles.
Student B Look at the information on page 119.
Student A You want to go to Manchester.

Now do the Stop and Check on page 50 of the Workbook.

UNIT 10

Used to – Question forms (2) – Question tags

The way we were

PRESENTATION

1 Molly Harrison was a young girl in the 1920s. Read what she says about it.

'We shocked our parents. We used to do things our mothers never did. We cut our hair, we wore short skirts, we smoked, and went dancing. I loved doing a dance called the Charleston. I once won a prize for that! My boyfriend had a car, a Model 'T' Ford. We often went for picnics in the countryside. The roads weren't busy then – no traffic jams! My father bought a car in 1925, an Austin Seven. He paid £150 for it! We went to the pictures twice a week, and it only cost sixpence. My favourite stars were Charlie Chaplin and Greta Garbo – the films were silent. I saw my first "talking" picture in 1927. Also, we listened to the radio a lot (the BBC started in 1922). I can remember it all so clearly.'

2 Look at the following examples of **used to**.
*We **used to** do things that shocked our parents.*
*She **used to** smoke* (but now she doesn't).
*He **didn't use to** like whisky* (but now he drinks it a lot).

> **Rule**
> **Used to** expresses a past habit or state which does not happen any more.
> *We **used to go** to the seaside every summer.*
> If the action happened once only, we can't use **used to**. We must use the Past Simple.
> *We **went** to Blackpool in 1929.*

3 Read the text about Molly and the 1920s again. Many sentences are possible with **used to**.
   a. Make some sentences with **used to** and **didn't use to**.
   b. Find five sentences where the verb forms *must* stay in the Past Simple.

4 **T.28a** Listen to Molly talking and notice the pronunciation of **used to** (/juːstʊ/ or /tə/). Practise saying the sentences.

71

PRACTICE

1 Listening and speaking

T.28b Linda Carr was a teenager in the 1960s. Listen to what she says about that time and answer the following questions using **used to** or the Past Simple.

1 What did she do that shocked her parents?
2 What did she do in 1965?
3 What did she and her friends do in their free time?
4 What did her parents do in their free time?
5 How did the students try to change the world?
6 What are some important dates from the '60s? What happened?

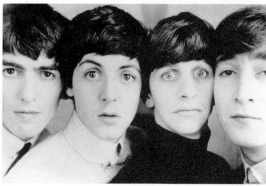

2 Speaking

Work in pairs.
Complete the table with information about your partner. Ask and answer questions about your lives now and when you were children.

> What do you do at the weekend?
>
> What did you do when you were a child?

> I (usually) do the shopping and . . .
>
> I used to play with my friends and . . .

Topic	Life now	Life as a child
What/do at the weekend?		
What/do in the morning?		
What/do in the evening?		
Where/go on holiday?		
What sports/play?		
What TV programmes/like?		
What newspapers/books/magazines/read?		
What food/like?		

3 Writing

Find out from your parents or other members of your family about life in your country when they were young. Write some sentences about it.

● Language review

Used to

A past habit or state can be expressed by **used to** + infinitive or the Past Simple. Actions which happened once are expressed by the Past Simple only. A present habit is expressed by the Present Simple, often with an adverb of frequency (**usually**, **sometimes**).

> **Translate**
>
> I used to smoke, but I never smoke now.
>
> He used to live in London, but he moved in 1990. Now he lives in Oxford.

▶ Grammar reference: page 128.

PRESENTATION

1 | **T.29** | Read and listen to the dialogue.

> **A** Who did you talk to at the party last night?
> **B** Oh, Jenny and Tom, but Jenny mainly.
> **A** What did you talk about?
> **B** She was telling me about her new job.
> **A** Who did you dance with?
> **B** No one. By the way, did you know that Belinda is going out with Steve?
> **A** No. Who told you that?
> **B** Tom did. Someone saw them together in a restaurant.
> **A** Who saw them?
> **B** Annie did.
> **A** Huh! You can't believe Annie!
> **B** Well, you don't know what Annie said.
> **A** Why? What happened in the restaurant?
> **B** Well, when Annie saw them, they were very surprised, and then they . . .

● Grammar questions

– Many verbs are used with a preposition (**write to**, **look at**, **listen to**). In the question, the preposition comes after the verb.

   What are you looking at?

   Find three questions like this in the dialogue.

– When **who** or **what** is the subject of the question, it comes immediately before the main verb.

   Who broke the window?

   Find three questions like this in the dialogue.

2 Listen to the dialogue again and practise the questions.

PRACTICE

1 Grammar

Put the words in the right order to form a question.

a. does/to/who/belong/pen/this?
b. are/about/thinking/you/what?
c. dream/did/last/you/about/night/what?
d. countries/have/to/been/which/you?
e. married/she/did/who/to/get?

Write questions with **who** or **what**.

f. John loves someone.
g. Someone loves John.
h. Peter had an argument with someone.
i. Something happened at the party.
j. Someone phoned last night.

2 Speaking and listening

Work in pairs.
Student A Look at the love story on this page.
Student B Look at the love story on page 119.
Ask each other questions to find out the missing information.

Example
George spoke to _____ . *Who did George speak to?*
_____ gave me a present. *Who gave you a present?*

Student A

A Love Story

George loves _____.
George phones Lily every day.
He sends her _____ every week.
George wrote a poem for Lily.
The poem was about _____.
One day George saw Lily in the park.
She was talking to _____.
James gave Lily some flowers.
James kissed _____.
Suddenly Lily saw George.
_____ hit James.
A policeman saw George.
The policeman took George to the _____. (Where?)
James drove Lily home.
Lily got married to _____.
George wrote a novel.
It was called _____.

● Language review

Subject questions

When **who** or **what** is the subject of the question, the verb has the same form as the statement. We do not use **do/does/did**.

George	loves Lily.

Who	loves Lily?

> **Translate**
>
> Who did George see?
>
>
> Who saw George?

▶ Grammar reference: page 128.

SKILLS DEVELOPMENT

● Reading and speaking

You are going to read an article about the time when women in Britain fought for the right to vote.

Pre-reading task

1 Look at the picture and read the introduction to the article.

Over 70 years ago, on 6 February 1918, the British Parliament passed an important law. This law gave women in Britain the right to vote for the first time. The right to vote is sometimes called suffrage. The women who fought for this right were called suffragettes. In many countries the women's fight was long and hard.

2 Work in pairs and answer the questions.
   a. Which country first gave women the right to vote? Was it America/Sweden/Switzerland/New Zealand?
   b. Which year was it? 1861/1893/1910?
   c. When did women in your country get the vote?

Reading and vocabulary

1 Read the article quickly and find four words that you don't know, and check them in your dictionary.
2 Compare with a partner the words you looked up.
3 Why is the title of the article 'Dying for the vote'? What are the two meanings of **dying for**?

Dying for the Vote

The suffragette movement started in the middle of the 19th century. Women de-
5 manded not only the right to vote, but also better education for girls. However, there was strong opposition. Many
10 men argued that women were less intelligent and more emotional than men, and therefore could not make important
15 decisions.

The first suffragettes believed in being legal a[nd] peaceful. They used to write letters to Parliament a[nd] organize petitions. Nothing happened. Nobody notic[ed] them.
20 By 1903, a woman called Emmeline Pankhurst a[nd] her daughters Christabel and Sylvia decided they need[ed] publicity for their cause. They encouraged women [to] break the law. Soon the newspapers were full of shocki[ng] stories about these new-style suffragettes.

Comprehension check

Now read the article more carefully. Choose the best answer, **a**, **b**, or **c**.

1 The suffragettes demanded
   a. other things as well as the right to vote.
   b. only the right to vote.
   c. a better education than men.
2 Emmeline Pankhurst encouraged women to break the law because
   a. she was tired of writing letters to Parliament.
   b. she wanted more publicity for the suffragettes.
   c. the first suffragettes did nothing.
3 Many women went to prison because
   a. they told shocking stories to the newspapers.
   b. they threw tomatoes and eggs at the crowds.
   c. they used to do things that were against the law.

25 **What did they do?**

They marched through the streets. They used to paint VOTES FOR WOMEN on walls, and break shop windows. Some women chained themselves to the railings outside Parliament and 10 Downing

30 Street. They had to be very courageous, because angry crowds came and threw tomatoes, eggs, and flour at them. Many women went to prison. There they refused to eat, and so prison officers used rubber tubes to force food into them.

35   The most shocking event was on Derby Day in June 1913. A suffragette called Emily Davidson ran in front of the King's horse and was killed. She was the first martyr for the cause.

    Gradually, opinion changed. Many members of

40 Parliament now wanted votes for women, but still nothing happened. During the First World War, women had to do men's jobs, and they did them well. It was only after this that women aged thirty and over got the vote. Ten more years passed before,

45 in 1928, women of twenty-one could vote.

4 Emily Davidson was a martyr because
  a. the King's horse killed her.
  b. she refused to eat and died.
  c. she shocked all the people at the Derby.

5 After the First World War
  a. Members of Parliament changed their opinions.
  b. women did men's jobs.
  c. women finally got the vote.

Discussion

Work in pairs. Discuss the following questions together, then tell the others in your class what you think.

1 What changes have there been in the roles of men and women in your country in the last 100 years?

2 In your opinion, what do women do better than men? What do men do better than women?

3 Are there any causes in your country or in the world that you feel strongly about? What are they?

● Vocabulary

Male and female words

Many words are used by both males and females to describe themselves and their possessions.

student   doctor   shoes   hat

Some nouns are used for either male or female, but not usually both.

Male	**Female**
waiter	*waitress*
tie	*dress*

1 Put the following words into the columns under the headings *Male/Female/Both*. Use your dictionary to check any words you don't know.

landlord   actor   bull   musician
teenager   cook   king   duke   guy
heroine   professor   nephew   uncle
bikini   pilot   dentist   niece   hero
model   skirt   duchess   queen
knickers   pyjamas   bra   scientist
architect   judge   cousin   cow
aunt   widow   underpants   athlete
blouse   actress   tourist   landlady
swimming trunks   widower   boots

Male	**Female**	**Both**

2 Who or what are the following?
  a. He's my sister's son. He's my _____ .
  b. The most important female character in a story is called the _____ .
  c. I wear these in bed. _____
  d. I run in races. I'm a/an _____ .
  e. I pay rent to him. He's my _____ .
  f. He wears these under his trousers. _____
  g. Her husband is dead. She's a/an _____ now.
  h. I check people's teeth. I'm a/an _____ .

3 Work in pairs.
Choose some other words from the columns above and write sentences to describe them.
Ask others in the class to tell you who or what it is.

● Listening and speaking

You are going to listen to two people who were born on the same day in the same year. They are now in their seventies. Their lives have been very different. Divide into two groups.

Group A

> **T.30a** You are going to listen to Bill Cole.

Group B

> **T.30b** You are going to listen to Camilla, the Duchess of Lochmar.

Listen once and say if you think he/she has had a happy life. Listen again and answer the following questions.

Comprehension check

1 When was he/she born?
2 Where did he/she use to live? What was his/her home like?
3 Did he/she have any brothers or sisters?
4 What does he/she say about the members of his/her family?
5 Did he/she have a good education?
6 What are his/her best memories?
7 How old was he/she when his/her father died? How did this change his/her life?
8 What jobs did he/she have?

When you have answered the questions, find a partner from the other group and compare the lives of Bill and Camilla. Who do you think has had the more interesting life?

● Everyday English

Question tags

1 **T.31** You will hear two conversations in a restaurant. Listen for the differences between them.

2 In spoken English, we often use question tags to invite people to agree with us, and to 'keep the conversation going'.

> **Man** *It's hot today, **isn't it**?*
> **Woman** *Yes, it is.*

Question tags like this aren't real questions at all. The man isn't telling the woman anything new – she knows it's hot! He is asking for her agreement, to be friendly and sociable and to 'make conversation'. In question tags like these, the intonation falls.

*It was cold yesterday, **wasn't it**?*

Listen to the first conversation again. How do we form question tags?

3 Ask your teacher for tapescript **31**. In pairs, practise the first conversation. Make sure your intonation falls on the question tags.

4 British people love talking about the weather! Complete the following conversations using one of the tags in the box.

has it?	is it?	isn't it?	didn't it?
haven't we?	doesn't it?	was it?	

Good weather

A Good morning! It's another lovely day, _____?

B It certainly is. It wasn't as warm as this yesterday, _____?

A No, it wasn't. It rained yesterday evening, _____?

B Yes. The sunshine makes you feel good, _____?

A You're absolutely right.

Bad weather

A Good morning! It isn't very warm today, _____?

B It certainly isn't. It hasn't been as cold as this for ages, _____?

A That's true. We've had some lovely weather recently, _____?

B Mm. Ah, well. Mustn't complain.

UNIT 11

Passives – Notices

Read all about it!

PRESENTATION

1 Complete the following sentences with the verb **to be** in the correct tense.
   a. They _are_ American. He _____ English.
   b. Last week they _____ in London, and he _____ in Chicago.
   c. She _____ _____ to Russia twice, but I _____ never _____ there.
   d. She _____ in New York next week.

   What are the names of the four tenses?

2 Write in the Past Simple and the Past Participles of the following verbs.
   Some are regular and some are irregular.

	Past Simple	Past Participle
sell	sold	sold
give		
buy		
produce		
drink		
build		
write		
grow		
steal		
invent		

3 Read the text below. It is the story of Coca-Cola, one of the world's most famous drinks.

Things go better with *Coca-Cola*

Coca-Cola is enjoyed all over the world. 1.6 billion gallons are sold every year, in over one hundred and sixty countries. The drink was invented by Dr John Pemberton in Atlanta, on 8 May 1886, but it was given the name Coca-Cola by his partner, Frank Robinson. In the first year, only nine drinks a day were sold.

The business was bought by a man called Asa Candler in 1888, and the first factory was opened in Dallas, Texas, in 1895. Coca-Cola is still made there. Billions of bottles and cans have been produced since 1895.

PHOTOGRAPH: PHILLIP VULLO

Diet Coke has been made since 1982, and over the years many clever advertisements have been used to sell the product. It is certain that Coca-Cola will be drunk far into the twenty-first century.

"Coca-Cola" and "Coke" are registered trademarks which identify the same product of The Coca-Cola Company.

Grammar questions

– What is the main interest of the text?
Dr John Pemberton? Frank Robinson? Coca-Cola?
– *1.6 billion gallons are sold every year.*
Do we know *who* sells Coca-Cola?
Is it important *who* sells it?

> **Rule**
> The subject of a sentence is usually what we are
> most interested in.
>   *Paper **is made** from wood.*
>   *This bridge **was built** in 1907.*
> In these sentences, we are not interested in *who*
> makes the paper, or *who* built the bridge.
> When we are more interested in the *object* of an
> active sentence than the *subject*, we use the passive.

4 All the verb forms in the text about Coca-Cola are in
the passive (except 'It is certain that . . .').
Complete this rule:
The passive is formed with the auxiliary verb _____
+ the _____ _____ .

PRACTICE

1 Writing and speaking

1 In the columns below, write in the passive verb forms
from the text on page 77.

Present Simple	Past Simple	Present Perfect	*Will* future
is enjoyed			

2 Don't look back at the text! Try to remember the
whole sentence!

> Coca-Cola is enjoyed all over the world.

3 Here are the answers to some questions. What are
the questions?
   – 1.6 billion gallons.
   – In 1886.
   – Only nine drinks a day. (*How much . . . ?*)
   – In Dallas.
   – Since 1982.

2 Grammar

Change the following sentences, active to passive or
passive to active.

Active	Passive
a. They make VW cars in Germany.	VW cars _____ in Germany.
b. They _____ rice in China.	Rice is grown in China.
c. Bell invented the telephone in 1876.	The telephone _____ by Bell in 1876.
d. Thieves _____ two pictures from the museum last night.	Two pictures were stolen from the museum last night.
e. They have built three new factories this year.	Three new factories _____ this year.
f. They _____ the picture for £3,000.	The picture has been sold for £3,000.
g. The factory will produce 10,000 cars next year.	10,000 cars _____ next year.
h. _____ they _____ many cars last year?	Were many cars made last year?
i. Bell didn't invent the television.	The television _____ by Bell.

3 Grammar and reading

Put the verbs in brackets in the correct tense, active or passive, to fit the meaning of the text.

NYLON
The first man-made fibre

NYLON (a)_____ (invent) in the early 1930s by an American chemist, Julian Hill. Other scientists (b)_____ (work) with his invention and finally on 27 October 1938, Nylon (c)_____ (introduce) to the world. It was cheap and strong and immediately (d)_____ (become) successful, especially in the making of ladies' stockings.

During the Second World War, the best present for many women was a pair of nylon stockings, but more importantly, it (e)_____ (use) to make parachutes and tyres.

Today, nylon (f)_____ (find) in many things: carpets, ropes, seat belts, furniture, computers, and even spare parts for the human body. It (g)_____ (play) an important part in our lives for over 50 years. Next year about 36 million tons of it (h)_____ (manufacture).

4 Writing

Complete the conversations with either a question or an answer.

> Are VWs made in Japan?

> No, they aren't. They're made in Germany.

> Is rice grown in England?

> No, it isn't. It's grown in tropical countries.

a. **A** Is Coca-Cola sold in many countries?
   B _____

b. **A** _____ ?
   B No, it wasn't. It was invented by Dr John Pemberton.

c. **A** Has Diet Coke been made for many years?
   B _____

d. **A** Was nylon invented after the Second World War?
   B _____

e. **A** _____ ?
   B Thirty-six million tons.

● Language review

The passive

In passive sentences, we are more interested in the object of the active sentence.
This is because *who did the thing* isn't important at the moment, or because we don't know *who did it*.
   *President Kennedy **was killed** in 1963.*
   *The Houses of Parliament **were built** between 1840 and 1857.*

Translate

The best cameras are made in Japan.

_____

My house was built in 1910.

_____

Ten pictures have been stolen from the National Gallery.

_____

A cure for cancer will soon be found.

_____

▶ **Grammar reference: page 129.**

SKILLS DEVELOPMENT

● Reading and speaking

Newspaper stories
When you read a newspaper, you never want to read all the articles and stories. Usually you check the headlines and just choose to read those articles which look interesting.

Pre-reading task
Look at these four newspaper headlines.

1 **HEART MAN ALIVE AND KICKING**

2 **CONCORDE'S BIRTHDAY**

3 **MILLION DOLLAR REWARD**

4 **£3 MILLION FOR A VET**

Use your dictionary to check vocabulary.

1 Which headlines do you think will have stories of interest to you?

2 Look at the following list of words. They all come from the stories that go with the headlines. Which words do you think go with which headline? Why?

fit (adj)	**spinster** (n)
graceful (adj)	**to train** (v) e.g. for a sport
honesty (n)	**transplant** (n)
lottery (n)	**wallet** (n)
mansion (n)	**will** (n) e.g. write a *will*
to operate (on sb) (v)	before you die
stable (n)	(to be) **worth** (adj)
speed (n)	

3 Choose one headline only. What do you want to know when you read the article? Write two questions.

Examples
Why did the man need a new heart?
How old is Concorde?
What did the person do to get a million dollars?
Why did the vet get £3 million?

Reading
Now read the story for the headline you chose.

---

1 **HEART MAN ALIVE AND KICKING**

BUILDER Phil Young is celebrating a very special anniversary today – it is exactly one year since he was 5 operated on at St Bartholomew's hospital and given a new heart.

Mr Young, 47, of Tottenham, is now so full of 10 energy that he is training to play in a charity football match to raise money for the hospital's transplant programme. So far eleven 15 people have been given new hearts.

Mr Young wants to help others like himself. In 1990 he was seriously ill with heart 20 disease. He couldn't work, he couldn't climb the stairs, and he had two young sons to look after.

Now the boys are helping 25 to train their father for the football match. 'My boys are very pleased that I am so fit again,' said Mr Young. 'I have become a real father to them 30 again. We don't just play football – we go jogging and swimming and play snooker together. I hope more people will be helped by the 35 hospital, as I was.'

Comprehension check

1 Which words from exercise **2** did you find in your article?

2 Did you find the answers to your questions?

3 Here are sixteen questions, four for each story. Find the four questions for your story and answer them.

   a. Why is it a special anniversary for Phil Young?
   b. Did France develop Concorde alone?
   c. Why is Peter Pocock a lucky man?
   d. Why is William Murphy a lucky man?
   e. Why is Mr Young training to play football?
   f. How many hours testing was Concorde given?
   g. Why are Miss de Beaumont's family furious?
   h. What did Mr Murphy do with the wallet?
   i. What can Mr Young do now that he couldn't do in 1990?
   j. Did Mr and Mrs Pocock expect to get Miss de Beaumont's money?
   k. When Mr Murphy saw he had the winning ticket, did he go to Mr Dupont's house immediately?
   l. In what ways is Mr Young a real father again?
   m. How is it possible to begin work in New York before you leave London?
   n. What do Mr and Mrs Pocock hope to do?
   o. When did Mr Dupont believe that he was a millionaire?
   p. Why was Ethel Lee a special passenger?

CONCORDE'S BIRTHDAY

CONCORDE, the world's fastest and most graceful passenger plane, will soon be 25 years old. It first flew on 2
5 March 1969, from Toulouse in France.

Concorde was developed by both France and Britain. From 1956 these two countries had a
10 dream of a supersonic passenger plane. In 1962 they started to work together on the project. The plane cost over £1.5 billion to develop. It is the
15 most tested plane in the history of aviation. It was given over 5,000 hours of testing.

Concorde flies at twice the speed of sound. This means
20 that it takes only 3 hours 25 minutes to fly between London and New York, compared with 7–8 hours in other passenger jets. Because of the five-hour
25 time difference between the USA and Britain, it is possible to travel west on Concorde and arrive in New York before you leave London! You can catch
30 the 10.30am flight from London, Heathrow and start work in New York an hour earlier!

Concorde is much used by
35 business people and film stars. But its oldest passenger was Mrs Ethel Lee from Leicestershire in England. She was 99 years old when she took
40 off from Heathrow on 24 February 1985.

Each Concorde is built at a cost of £55 million. Twenty have been built so far. Air
45 France and British Airways own the most. They each have seven planes.

£3 MILLION FOR A VET

VET Peter Pocock has been left a fortune by a spinster whose horses and dogs he looked after.
5 The 90-year-old spinster, Miss Marguerite de Beaumont, was helped in other ways by Mr Pocock. He cleaned and tidied her 11-room Elizabethan
10 mansion when she became too old and ill to care for it. When she died she left him everything in her will: her money, the house and gardens, her
15 stables – all of which is worth £3 million.

Miss de Beaumont's family are furious. Her niece, Mrs Charmian Pickford said 'We
20 are very upset. We are going to fight the will. My aunt didn't know what she was doing – she was senile in her last years.'

Mr Pocock, 42, lives in the
25 next village with his wife and baby daughter. They were

shocked by Miss de Beaumont's generosity. 'We can't believe it,' said Mrs Pocock, 'so much
30 money is wonderful, but will it make us happier? Money can bring problems. Our hope is that the mansion will be made beautiful again. Perhaps we
35 can do that now with the money.' Miss de Beaumont bought the mansion in 1934 and started a horse farm. It has not been looked after well for
40 many years, but the beauty of the buildings and the garden can still be seen.

MILLION DOLLAR REWARD

Mr William Murphy, from Montreal in Canada, now knows that honesty pays. Last Sunday he returned a lost
5 lottery ticket to its owner and he was given $1.2 million as a reward!

Last Thursday, Mr Murphy, aged 28 and unemployed,
10 found a wallet on a Montreal Street. It contained $85, some credit cards, and some lottery tickets. Mr Murphy checked the address in the wallet and
15 immediately posted it back to its owner, Mr Jean-Paul Dupont, but he didn't send the lottery tickets back. 'I kept the tickets. I wanted to check
20 them. I thought maybe I'd win $10 or something.'

On Sunday, Mr Murphy bought a newspaper and started checking the numbers
25 on the tickets. He couldn't believe it – he had the winning ticket! It was worth $7 million!

He thought about keeping the tickets and getting the
30 money for himself. He sat and thought about it for two hours, but he knew what he had to do. He took the bus to Mr Dupont's address and knocked
35 at the door. The door was opened not by Mr Dupont, but by his son, Yves, who doesn't speak English very well.

'Good evening,' said Mr
40 Murphy. 'Are you Mr Dupont?'
'Oui,' said Yves.
'Well, congratulations! You're a millionaire!'
'Uh?' said Yves.
45 Then his father came to the door. He understands English, but he didn't believe his ears until he was shown the lottery ticket and the newspaper.
50 'What an honest man!' he said. 'You deserve a reward – at least $1 million, I think.'

Jean-Paul Dupont thanks William Murphy, finder of the winning lottery ticket, in Montreal.

---

4 Find someone in the class who read the same story as you. Check your answers to the questions.
5 Find people who read different stories from you. Tell them about what you read.
6 Find some examples of passives in each story.

Further reading and speaking
If you can, get an English newspaper. Look through it quickly and choose one or two articles to read.
Tell the others in your class about them and why you chose them.

● Vocabulary

Words that go together

Use your dictionaries to help you. Work in pairs.

1 Verbs and nouns that go together
In each of the boxes below, one or two of the nouns do *not* go with the verb in the middle. Draw a line to show which nouns *can* go with the verb.

£1,000		a competition
a bank a wallet		a war John McEnroe
steal		**win**
ear-rings a post office		£10,000 a football match
a bus		ear-rings
a fish a train		a seat belt a briefcase
catch		**wear**
a cold a thief		a watch a uniform
a car		an umbrella
a poem		tennis
a lie the truth		the piano cards
tell		**play**
a joke a story		a competition swimming

Practice
Write two sentences for each verb using some of the correct nouns.

Examples
*The thieves **stole** my mother's **ear-rings** from her bedroom.*
*I **won** a **competition** in a newspaper.*
*The policeman wasn't **wearing** his **uniform**.*

2 Words and prepositions that go together
Put a preposition into each gap.
a. I always laugh _____ his jokes.
b. The doctor operated _____ the patient.
c. He suffers _____ bad headaches.
d. The head teacher is ill, so Mrs Betts is _____ charge today.
e. Do you know what's _____ TV tonight?
f. 'Shall we go for a picnic tomorrow?' 'It depends _____ the weather.'
g. I'm really bored _____ my job.
h. I wasn't invited _____ the party.
i. Kate is _____ love _____ Thomas.
j. We're going _____ holiday to Italy next year.
k. I'm very sorry. I broke it _____ accident.
l. Who does this book belong _____ ?

There is a list of words + preposition on page 142.

● Listening and speaking

The world's most loved car
You are going to listen to a radio programme about the world's most loved car, the Volkswagen Beetle.

Pre-listening task
Use your dictionary to check words you don't know.
1 What is the meaning of the word *beetle*?
   What is the Beetle called in your country?
2 The following words are used in the programme.
   reliable (*adj*)   **to chat** (*v*)   **fan** (*n*)
   jolly (*adj*)   **to design** (*v*)   **to wave** (*v*)
   Put them in the correct gaps in the sentences below.
   Put the verbs in the correct form.
   a. This church _____ by Wren in 1670.
   b. He's a big _____ of Tina Turner.
   c. She's a very _____ friend. She's always there when you need her.
   d. 'Did you talk to Pat much?' 'No, we just _____ for a few minutes.'
   e. Her uncle's a _____ man. He's always laughing.
   f. That's Penny over there. Look! She's _____ at us.

Listening

T.32 Listen to the programme. Make sentences about the VW Beetle, using the six words in exercise 2 opposite. What does *Volkswagen* mean?

Comprehension check

Are the following statements true or false?
If false, say why.
1 People like Beetles because they are so comfortable.
2 The man feels that his car is his friend.
3 His friends who own Beetles have thought of lots of ways to improve their cars.
4 Ferdinand Porsche was asked to design the car in 1938.
5 American and British soldiers in Germany didn't like the Beetle cars very much.
6 Some Beetles were taken back to Britain and America by the soldiers.
7 Peter Baber opened the first VW garage in America in the 1950s.
8 His father started a magazine for people who owned or liked Beetles.
9 Peter Baber's schoolfriends first called the car a Beetle.
10 No Beetles have been made in the world since 1974.

What do you think?

1 What is the message of the song? Can you remember (sing!) any of it?
2 What is your favourite car? Why?
3 Which other cars do you know that are loved in the same way as Beetles? Which modern cars do you think will be loved as much in the future?

● Everyday English

Notices

1 When you first go to a foreign country, reading notices can be difficult. Here are some typical English notices. Match each notice with a place below.

a.
10.55 EDINBURGH
calling at
YORK
NEWCASTLE

b.
FOREIGN EXCHANGE

c.
VICTORIA LINE
SOUTHBOUND

d.
Afternoon Tea Served

e.

please have the EXACT fare ready

f.
UNDER 18s WILL NOT BE SERVED

g.
engaged

h.
EEC Passport Holders Only

i.
keep your **distance**

j.
PLEASE DO NOT FEED THE ANIMALS

k.

OUT OF ORDER

l.
NO CYCLING ON THE FOOTPATHS

m.
QUEUE THIS SIDE PLEASE

1 A bank	___	8 A park	___
2 Outside a cinema	___	9 A zoo	___
3 A drinks machine	___	10 A hotel	___
4 A bus	___	11 A railway station	___
5 An airport	___	12 A public toilet	___
6 A pub	___	13 A motorway	___
7 The Underground	___		

2 **T.33** You will hear five short recordings. Where are the dialogues taking place?

3 Work in pairs.

Choose two other places, and write conversations that could happen there. Tell the rest of the class, and see if they can guess the place.

UNIT 12

Verb patterns (2) – Apostrophes – Time

Adventure!

PRESENTATION

1 There is a feature in a magazine called 'It happened to me', where readers are invited to write about something extraordinary that has happened to them. Read about Tony Russell.

It happened to me

Tony Russell describes how the sight of a tiger in Nepal – '500 kilos plus and four metres long' – will stay with him forever.

THE DAY I CAME FACE TO FACE WITH A TIGER

Last year I went to Nepal for three months to work in a hospital. I think it's important to see as much of a country as you can, but it is difficult to travel around Nepal. The hospital let me have a few days' holiday, so I decided to go into the jungle and I asked a Nepalese
10 guide, Kamal Rai, to go with me.

We started preparing for the trip at six in the morning, and left camp with two elephants carrying our equipment. It was hot, but Kamal made me wear shoes and trousers to
15 protect me from snakes. In the jungle there was a lot of wildlife, but we were trying to find big cats, especially tigers. We climbed onto the elephants' backs to get a better view, but it is unusual to find tigers in the afternoon because
20 they sleep in the heat of the day.

Then, in the distance, we saw a tiger, and Kamal told me to be very quiet. We crept nearer and found a dead deer, still bleeding. This was the tiger's lunch! Suddenly I started to feel very
25 frightened.

We heard the tiger a second before we saw it. It jumped out like a flash of lightning, five hundred kilos plus and four metres long. I looked into its eyes and face, and saw right down the animal's
30 throat. It grabbed Kamal's leg between its teeth, but I managed to pull Kamal away. One of our elephants ran at the tiger and made it go back into the grass, so we quickly escaped to let the tiger eat its lunch. That night it was impossible to sleep!

2 Answer the questions.

   a. Why did Tony go to Nepal?
   b. What does he think it's important to do abroad?
   c. Is transport good in Nepal?
   d. Did the hospital let him have a long holiday?
   e. Who did he ask to go with him into the jungle?
   f. What did the guide make him wear? Why?
   g. Why did they climb onto the elephants?
   h. How did Kamal escape?

● Grammar questions

– In the text, there are two examples of the verb pattern **ask/tell somebody to do** (something).
> *He asked her to dance.*

Find them.

– There are four examples of the pattern **make/let somebody do** (something).
> *You make me laugh!*

Find them. What is the difference between **make** and **let**?

– Find the examples of the following verbs.
> *decided   started* (×2)   *trying   managed*

Are they followed by an infinitive or an **-ing** form?

– There are four examples of the pattern adjective + infinitive.
> *It's easy to learn English.*

Find them.

– There are four examples of the infinitive used to express purpose.
> *I come to class to learn English.*

Find them.

PRACTICE

1 Grammar

1 Put a form of **make** or **let** and a suitable verb into each gap.

Example
*The teacher **let** me **go** home early because I felt ill.*

   a. My children usually go to bed early, but I _____ them _____ TV till 10.00 at the weekend.
   b. I don't like the sight of blood. It _____ me _____ ill if I see it.
   c. My parents weren't strict with me at all. They _____ me _____ what I wanted.
   d. But they thought that education was very important, so they _____ me _____ hard for my exams.
   e. It was a very sad film. The ending _____ me _____ .
   f. My parents _____ me _____ the piano for two hours every day. I hate it.
   g. My brother _____ me _____ his car sometimes, but I have to pay for the petrol.

Think of your favourite teacher, and a teacher you don't/didn't like!

> He lets us play games.

> She made us do homework every night!

85

2 Rewrite the following sentences using **tell** or **ask**.

Example
'Can you help me?' she said to him.
*She **asked** him to help her.*

a. 'Can you lend me some money?' I asked her.

_____

b. 'Do your homework again,' the teacher said to me.

_____

c. 'Please write to me soon,' I said to her.

_____

d. 'Do more exercise,' the doctor said to Peter.

_____

e. 'Drive more carefully!' she said to me.

_____

What are some of the things your parents tell/told/ask/asked you to do?

> They asked me to do the shopping sometimes.

> They tell me to tidy my room.

3 Choose the correct form of the verb.

buying ☐
a. Let me buy ☐ you a drink.
to buy ☐

stop ☐
b. I've decided stopping ☐ smoking.
to stop ☐

to find ☐
c. I managed finding ☐ the book I was looking for.
find ☐

to think ☐
d. The smell of roses makes me think ☐ of you.
thinking ☐

understanding ☐
e. I tried understand ☐ the lecture, but it was too difficult.
to understand ☐

to do ☐
f. The doctor told me doing ☐ more exercise.
do ☐

snow ☐
g. Look outside! It's starting snowing ☐
to snow ☐

2 Speaking

Work in pairs. Ask and answer questions about why you go to certain places.

> Why do you go to a hairdresser's?

> To have a haircut.

– post office   – petrol station
– book shop   – newsagent's
– library   – butcher's
– travel agent's – off-licence

3 Apostrophes

1 Apostrophes are used to show where letters are left out.
   can't   she's   I'd
They are also used to show possession.
   Helen's book   the girls' room (more than one girl)
   a day's holiday   four days' holiday
Find examples of both uses in the text on page 84.

2 Is the apostrophe used correctly in the following phrases? Correct any mistakes.
   – Kamals' leg   – my parent's house
   – Its raining.   – I went to a boy's school
   – two day's holiday   – I looked down its throat.

3 Put apostrophes in the following sentences.
   a. My childrens favourite game is chasing Wally the cat. Its not a game I like, and the cat certainly doesnt like it. It hides under Kates bed, or runs up its favourite tree, where the children cant get it.

   b. 'Have you seen todays newspaper?'
   'No, I havent. Why?'
   'Were going on holiday to America in a few days time, and I wondered what the weathers been like.'

86

4 Speaking

Work in pairs.
Using the following words and pictures to help you, retell the story about Tony Russell.

Tony Russell / go / Nepal / work / hospital

hospital / let / have a few days' holiday / decide / go / jungle / ask / guide / come

start / prepare / 6.00 / Kamal / make / wear / shoes and trousers / protect him from snakes

climb / elephants' backs / get / view

see / tiger / Kamal / tell him / quiet / start / feel / frightened

tiger / jump out / look down / throat

grab / Kamal's leg / manage / pull Kamal away

elephant / run at tiger / escape / impossible / sleep

● Language review

Verb patterns

We saw in Unit 5 that verbs can be followed by an infinitive. Here are some more.

I've decided
I'm trying | **to stop** smoking.
I managed

She told me
She asked me | **to ring** her.

He made me **cry**.
She lets me **do** what I want.

> **Translate**
>
> She told me to ring her.
> _____
>
> She asked me to ring her.
> _____
>
> He made me cry.
> _____
>
> She lets me do what I want.
> _____

There is a list of verb patterns on page 143.

Infinitives

Infinitives are used after certain adjectives.

It's | *easy* / *difficult* | **to learn** languages.

> **Translate**
>
> It's difficult to read your writing.

Infinitives are also used to express purpose.

*I went to Nepal **to work** as a doctor.*

> **Translate**
>
> I come to class to learn English.

▶ **Grammar reference: page 129.**

SKILLS DEVELOPMENT

● Reading and speaking

National heroes

Pre-reading task

You are going to read about two legendary English heroes, King Arthur and Robin Hood. (A legend is an old, popular story which is perhaps true and perhaps not.)

1 Look at the pictures and answer the questions.
When do you think they lived?
Where did they live? (In a house/a hut?)
Who did they fight against?
What weapons did they fight with?
2 What is happening in the pictures?
Do you know any stories about King Arthur or Robin Hood?

Vocabulary

Match a line in **A** with a line in **B** to define the words in italics.

A	B
When you *bring up* children,	in a hole in the ground when they are dead.
A *battle* is	you take them prisoner.
If you *defeat* your enemy,	you are badly hurt.
If you *capture* someone,	was a soldier who rode a horse.
If you are *wounded* in a battle,	you look after them and educate them until they are grown up.
In medieval times, a *knight*	the place where you bury someone.
You *bury* someone	a fight between soldiers, armies, etc.
A *tomb* is	you win a victory over them in a battle.

Jigsaw reading

Divide into two groups.
Group A Read about King Arthur.
Group B Read about Robin Hood.
Answer the questions as you read.

Comprehension check

1 When did stories about him begin to appear?
2 Who is the legend based on?
3 When did he live?
4 Where did he live?
5 He was the leader of a group of people. Who were they? What did they use to do?
6 Was he a good man?
7 Why is he famous? What are some of the things he did?
8 Who were his enemies?
9 How did he die?

When you have answered your questions, find a partner from the other group.
Compare your answers and swap information.
Read both texts, and find examples of the grammar taught in this unit (verb patterns and infinitives to express purpose).

Speaking

1 What do King Arthur and Robin Hood have in common?
2 Your teacher has information about two real English heroines, Florence Nightingale and Amy Johnson. Ask your teacher questions to find out about them.
3 Who are the legendary or real heroes and heroines from your country?
4 Are there certain 'ingredients' that legends have in common?

KING ARTHUR

The legends of King Arthur began to appear in the twelfth century, and it is possible that they are based on a Celtic leader in the fifth or sixth century who defended his country against Saxon invasion. King Arthur was the son of Pendragon, and was born in Tintagel in Cornwall. He was brought up by Merlin, an old Celtic magician, and became king of Britain when he was fifteen. He proved his right to be king when he managed to pull a sword from a rock. He had to fight many lords, and when, with Merlin's help, he defeated them, he received the magic sword *Excalibur* from the Lady of the Lake. He married Guinevere and lived in a castle at Camelot. His knights sat at a round table so that they were all equal – nobody was sitting at the head of the table. Many of the stories in the legends are about the adventures of the knights, among them Lancelot, Perceval, Gawain, and Galahad. They spent their time hunting wild pigs, having feasts, and singing ballads. They often had to kill dragons and giants. At all times they behaved very correctly, with respect, honour, and compassion.

Arthur went to Rome to fight the emperor, Lucius, and he left his kingdom in the hands of his nephew, Modred. As he was entering Rome, Arthur learned that Modred had taken control of the kingdom and had captured Guinevere. He came back to England and defeated his nephew, but in the battle was seriously wounded. Arthur told Sir Belvedere, the last surviving knight, to throw *Excalibur* into the water of a lake. He did this, and the sword was caught by a hand which came out of the water and then took the sword below the surface.

Arthur was then taken to the Isle of Avalon to get better. We understand that he did not die, but lives on and will return when his country needs him. The legend says that the following verse is written on his tomb:

HIC IACET ARTHURUS,
REX QUONDAM
REXQUE FUTURUS

(HERE LIES ARTHUR, THE ONCE AND FUTURE KING).

ROBIN HOOD

Robin Hood is a legendary hero who lived in Sherwood Forest, in Nottingham, with his band of followers. Stories about him and his adventures began to appear in the fourteenth century, but the facts behind the legend are uncertain. One writer thinks Robin was born in 1160, at a time when there were many robbers living in the woods, stealing from the rich but only killing in self-defence.

Everyone knows that Robin Hood robbed the rich to give to the poor. He chose to be an outlaw, that is, someone who lives 'outside the law', but he had his own ideas of right and wrong. He fought against injustice, and tried to give ordinary people a share of the riches owned by people in authority and the Church. He had many qualities – he was a great sportsman, a brave fighter, and was very good with his bow and arrow.

He dressed in green, lived in the forest with his wife, Maid Marion, and his men, among them Friar Tuck, Allen a Dale, Will Scarlet, and Little John. For food, they killed the King's deer, and many days were spent eating, drinking, and playing games. He robbed the rich by capturing them as they travelled through the forest and inviting them to eat with him. During the supper, someone looked in their bags to see how much money they had. When it was finished, Robin asked them to pay for the meal, and of course, he knew how much to ask for!

His main enemy was the Sheriff of Nottingham, who was always trying to capture Robin but never managed to do it. Some stories say that he killed Robin by poisoning him. In his dying moments, he shot a final arrow from his famous bow, and asked Little John to bury him where the arrow landed.

● Vocabulary

Adverbs

1 We do not usually put adverbs between a verb and its object.

Examples
You speak English well. (*Not* You speak well English.)
I like reading very much. (*Not* I like very much reading.)
I did my homework quickly. (*Not* I did quickly my homework.)

Some adverbs can move position:

Yesterday it rained all day.
It rained all day yesterday. (There is little difference.)

Some sound best in just one position:

Suddenly a tiger appeared. (It is more dramatic to have **suddenly** at the beginning.)

2 Put one of the adverbs into each gap. Sometimes more than one adverb is possible.

quickly	slowly	carefully	heavily
patiently	clearly	seriously	suddenly
badly	fluently	properly	
well/hard (irregular)			

a. I can't see _____ without my glasses.

b. They escaped from the tiger as _____ as possible.

c. Three people were _____ injured in a car crash.

d. I used to speak French _____, but I've forgotten it.

e. I read the letter _____ .

f. She worked _____ all weekend.

g. When I left work, it was raining _____ .

h. I waited _____ in the traffic jam, because I knew there was nothing I could do about it.

i. I was driving home when _____ I ran out of petrol.

j. I drove _____, because the conditions were bad.

k. She explained the problem _____ .

l. I did _____ in my driving test and passed first time.

m. I couldn't fill in the form _____, because I didn't have all the information.

-ed and -ing adjectives

1 We can use past participles to say how we feel about something.
*I'm very **interested** in modern art.*
*I was so **excited** that I couldn't sleep.*
We use the **-ing** form to talk about the thing or person that makes us feel interested or excited, etc.
*That picture is very **interesting**.*
*Skiing is an **exciting** sport.*

2 Put one of the adjectives into each gap. Sometimes more than one is possible.

interested/interesting	bored/boring
embarrassed/embarrassing	tired/tiring
surprised/surprising	

a. Your news was very _____ . I'm pleased you're enjoying yourself.

b. I liked the book until the end. It had a _____ ending which I didn't like.

c. A   How was your journey?
B   Very _____ . I think I'll go to bed.

d. The play was so _____ that I fell asleep.

e. He started to tell a joke about the director when the director came into the room. It was very _____ .

f. You look _____ . Have you had a busy day?

g. It's Sunday and I don't know what to do. I'm _____ .

h. Are you _____ in museums? I'm going to the National this afternoon – do you want to come?

3 What films have you seen recently? What books have you read? What did you think of them?

> I read a spy novel. It was very exciting.

> I saw a horror film. I thought it was frightening.

Listening

Pre-listening task

1 What stories do you know about UFOs (Unidentified Flying Objects)?
2 Some people say they have seen flying saucers. What do they say they look like? Draw one!
3 You are going to listen to a man who says he has seen a UFO, spoken to the aliens in it and been inside their space craft. What would you like to ask him?

> Where were you?
> Did they speak to you?

Listening for information

T.34 Listen to the interview and look at the pictures. Put them in the right order. There is one mistake in each picture. Find the eight mistakes.

Comprehension check

1 Which of your questions did Mr Burton answer?
2 What do the following refer to in the story?

Example
about a year ago – *He saw the UFO about a year ago.*

- one o'clock
- three hundred feet
- full moon
- five feet away
- ten or fifteen seconds
- green
- a machine
- black
- red
- five minutes
- two o'clock

3 Retell Mr Burton's story, beginning like this:
One night, Mr Burton decided to go fishing because. . .

What do you think?

1 The interview was based on a book of scientific research into UFOs by Timothy Good. He quotes many officials, including a former member of the Chief of Defence Staff, pilots, and astronauts, who say they have seen UFOs. Timothy Good thinks that so many reliable people have seen UFOs that they *must* exist. Also, stories from all over the world are remarkably similar. Common ideas are:
 - the space ships are round, fly very fast, and make no noise
 - they have bright lights and a shiny, metallic surface
 - they are often seen at night near military bases
 - the aliens are smaller than us, wear tight, one-piece uniforms, have larger heads but similar faces
 - the aliens are not violent.
 How much is this similar to Mr Burton's story?

2 Timothy Good thinks that the officials are not telling the truth. Do you agree?
 Why might officials not tell the truth?

3 His book concludes 'I believe that Man's progress on Earth has been watched by beings whose technological and mental developments make ours look primitive'.
 What do you think?

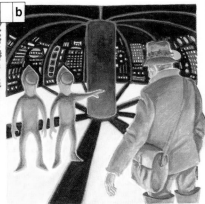

Speaking

Work in groups of four. Write a short story about the time when someone meets an alien. Look at the ingredients below to give you some ideas.

Place	Time
in the garden at home in a country lane in a plane at 30,000 feet in an Inca town	in the middle of the night in the year 2050 last night in the fifteenth century
People	**Events**

characters with five heads
talking machines
green beings from
    invisible planets
time travellers
	space ships travelling at
	    the speed of light
	visits to other galaxies
	getting lost in black holes
	planet Earth is an
	    experiment

● Everyday English

Time

1 There are several ways of telling the time.
   past/to
   It's twenty past six.
   It's a quarter past eight.
   It's half past ten.
   It's ten to three.
   It's a quarter to four.
   With **five**, **ten**, **twenty**, and **twenty-five**, we do not say 'minutes'. With all other numbers, we do.
   It's four minutes past two.
   It's twenty-eight minutes past six.
   It's twelve minutes to four.
   hour + minutes
   It's 6.20. (six twenty)
   It's 10.30. (ten thirty)
   It's 3.50. (three fifty)
   It's 2.04. (two oh four – 'O' is pronounced /əʊ/)
   It's 6.28. (six twenty-eight)
   It's 3.48. (three forty-eight)

2 We do not usually use the twenty-four hour clock when we speak. If we want to be specific, we add **in the morning/in the afternoon/at night**, or **a.m./p.m.**
   I got home at four o'clock in the morning/4.00 a.m.

   The twenty-four hour clock is used in timetables and announcements.
   The BA flight to New York leaves at fifteen forty.

3 [**T.35**] You will hear twelve short recordings. In each one there is a time. Write down the time you hear.

4 Say these times in different ways.

5 Work in pairs. Ask each other questions.
   Example
   What time do you go to bed?

92

Now do the Stop and Check on page 64 of the Workbook.

UNIT 13

Dreams and reality

PRESENTATION

1 Read about how Tanya describes her life and her dream.

Tanya, aged 7
I live in a block of flats with my Mum and little brother. My Mum works in a hospital, and so my Gran often looks after us and helps my Mum. We have a budgie and a goldfish. I go to St Paul's School and I wear a blue and grey uniform.

If . . . If I were a princess, I'd live in a palace. If I lived in a palace, I'd have servants to look after me. My Mum would be Queen, and she wouldn't work. I wouldn't go to school, I'd have a governess. I'd ride a white horse and I'd wear a long dress and a gold crown.

● Grammar questions

– Which tense is used to describe Tanya's real life?
– *If I lived in a palace, . . .*
  Does she live in a palace?
  What tense is **lived**?
– *. . . I'd have servants to look after me.*
  Is this a dream or reality?
– Complete the following rule.
  The Second Conditional is formed with **if** + the
  _____ tense, the auxiliary verb _____ + the
  _____ without **to**.

2 Practise the sentences that express Tanya's dream.

3 Read about how Graham describes his life, and complete the sentences about his dream.

Graham, aged 9
I live in a cottage in a village near Glasgow. My Dad is unemployed and my Mum works in a pub in the city. I go to the village school. I walk to school with my friend. We often play football together. I have a cat and some chickens.

If . . . If I _____ a prince, I _____ in a castle. I _____ in a cottage. My Dad _____ King, and my Mum _____ in a pub. A chauffeur _____ me to school. I _____ polo on a white horse. I _____ peacocks in my garden. I _____ chickens.

4 Answer these questions about Tanya. Use short answers.

If Tanya were a princess, . . .
– where would she live? *In a palace.*
– would her Gran look after her? *No, she wouldn't. Servants would.*
  a. who would be Queen?
  b. would her Mum work?
  c. would Tanya go to school?
  d. would she have any pets?
  e. what would she wear?

Ask and answer similar questions about Graham.

Example
Graham/live/castle?

Would Graham live in a castle? Yes, he would.

  f. he/live/cottage?
  g. his mother/work/pub?
  h. Who/take/him/school?
  i. What sport/he/play?
  j. he/have/chickens?

PRACTICE

1 Grammar

1 Make sentences from charts **A** and **B**.

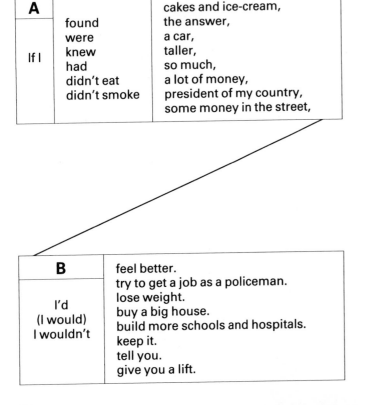

A		
If I	found were knew had didn't eat didn't smoke	cakes and ice-cream, the answer, a car, taller, so much, a lot of money, president of my country, some money in the street,

B	
I'd (I would) I wouldn't	feel better. try to get a job as a policeman. lose weight. buy a big house. build more schools and hospitals. keep it. tell you. give you a lift.

2 Put the verbs in the correct form, Past Simple or **would**.
  a. If I _____ (be) rich, I _____ (travel) around the world.
  b. I don't like Hollywood. I _____ (not live) there if I _____ (be) a film star.
  c. I _____ (go) to work if I _____ (not feel) so ill, but I feel awful.
  d. What _____ you do if your baby _____ (fall) into the water?
  e. If I _____ (have) more free time, I _____ (not waste) it. I _____ (learn) another language.

3 Finish these sentences in a suitable way.
  a. If I won £10,000, . . .
  b. If I spoke perfect English, . . .
  c. If I were on holiday, . . .

2 Speaking

Work in pairs. Imagine yourselves in the following situations, and discuss what you would do.

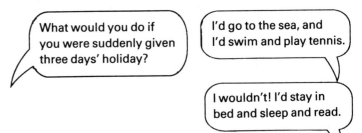
What would you do if you were suddenly given three days' holiday? I'd go to the sea, and I'd swim and play tennis. I wouldn't! I'd stay in bed and sleep and read.

What would you do if . . .
– your mother bought you a sweater for your birthday and you didn't like it?
– you were at a friend's house for dinner, and you didn't like the food?
– you came home and found a burglar?
– you saw someone stealing from a shop?

● Language review

Second Conditional

Read the Language review about the First Conditional on page 67 again. The Second Conditional expresses an unreal situation and its results.

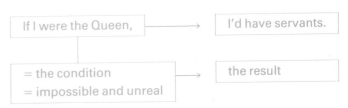
If I were the Queen, → I'd have servants.
= the condition → the result
= impossible and unreal

▶ **Grammar reference: page 130.**

PRESENTATION

1 Alan and Mike are eighteen-year-old twins. They have just left school. Read what they say about their future careers.

Alan
'Well, first I'm having a holiday. I'm travelling round Europe for the summer, and then in October I'm going to university to study business and marketing. I've always wanted to work in management. By the time I'm twenty-five, I want to be very rich, so after university I'm going to work in the City with my father. He's a stockbroker.'

Mike
'I know it's time for decisions, but I'm not very good at decisions. I might go to university, but I'm not sure. I might wait and travel around the Far East for a while.
After that, I might become a teacher. I know you don't earn much, but I like working with kids. Someone told me there are a lot of jobs teaching English so I might do a course in that. Then I could teach and travel!'

● Grammar questions

– Who is sure about what he wants to do? Who isn't sure?
– What future forms does Alan use?
– Which verb does Mike use that shows he isn't sure about his future career?

2 Complete the sentences about Alan and Mike. Use **he**, not **I**.

Example
Alan/travel round Europe
Alan's travelling round Europe for the summer.

a. university/October/business and marketing
b. After university/work/City/father
c. Mike/university/but/not sure
d. travel/Far East
e. become a teacher
f. do a course to teach English

PRACTICE

1 Speaking

Work in pairs.
Student A Ask about **B**'s plans.
Student B You aren't sure!

Example
doing tonight?
go out/stay at home

> What are you doing tonight?

> I don't know. I might go out, or I might stay at home.

a. A What sort of car/going to buy?
B Ford/Honda
b. A Where/on holiday?
B America/India
c. A What colour/going to paint/bedroom?
B blue/yellow
d. (in a restaurant)
A What/going to have?
B steak/fish
e. (It's **B**'s birthday soon.)
A What/going to do/birthday?
B theatre/invite a few friends round

Now ask and answer for yourselves! Ask about:
– after the lesson   – at the weekend
– this evening   – for your next holiday

2 Grammar

1 Choose the correct verb form in the following sentences.
  a. 'What's for supper?'
    '*We're having/we might have* lamb. It's in the oven.'
  b. 'What time are we eating?'
    '7.00. Don't worry. *It'll be ready/it might be ready* before your TV programme.'
  c. 'Who's coming for supper?'
    'I invited Jerry, but he *will be/might be* late. It depends on the traffic.'
  d. 'What are you doing tomorrow?'
    'I don't know yet. *I'm going/I might go* into town.'

2 Correct the mistakes in the following sentences.
  a. If I would have a car, I would give you a lift.
  b. They will call the new baby Victoria, but they aren't sure yet.
  c. My sister would visit us more often if she wouldn't live so far away.
  d. I'm playing tennis tomorrow, but I'm not sure.
  e. If I'm younger, I'll learn to play the piano, but I'm too old now.

● Language review

Might

Might is used to express the possibility that something will happen. It means the same as **will perhaps**.

> **Translate**
>
> Take your umbrella. It might rain.
>
> _____

▶ Grammar reference: page 130.

SKILLS DEVELOPMENT

● Reading and speaking

The dream game

Pre-reading task
Work in small groups and discuss the following:
1 Did you dream last night?
  Can you remember what you dreamt about?
2 Do you often dream? Do you often have the same dream? Describe your memorable dreams.
3 Do you think dreams are important? If so, why?

Playing the dream game
1 Read the introduction to the dream game. Do you agree with what the writer says about dreaming?
2 Play the dream game in pairs or small groups. Take turns to read the questions aloud. Make a note of your answers, then compare them. Use your dictionary if necessary.
3 Read the interpretation.
4 Discuss with the whole class. Do you agree or disagree with the interpretation of your personality?

The Dream Game

Introduction

Some people say that they never dream. But that is not possible. Everybody has dreams, but some people just have a better memory for them than others. Every one and a half hours throughout the night we live our private fantasies in our dreams — we can forget the good behaviour of the day and we are free to behave in any way we want. Images from our past and present come together. But as soon as we wake, the dream starts to melt, and the more we try to remember the details, the more we forget.

'I had this amazing dream last night. I must tell you about it — now, I was in my old school, er . . . but it wasn't a school, it was . . . er . . . it was a kind of a . . . er . . . I don't really know what it was.'

So, why do we dream? Are dreams important? The experts tell us that they are, because they can help us prepare for the problems of everyday life. The images in our dreams have special meaning, and they can help us to understand our inner personality.

Play the dream game

1 You are asleep and you are dreaming. In your dream you find yourself in your perfect house. What is it like? Describe it in detail.
2 Now you are walking along a narrow path. Suddenly you find a cup/glass/drinking vessel on the ground in front of you. What is it like? What is in it?
3 Now the path ends and you are walking in a wood. You walk quite a long way until you find a clearing. In the middle of the clearing is a building. What sort of building is it?
4 Around the building is a garden. Describe the garden.
5 You walk out of the garden and through the wood. At the edge of the wood there is a wall. The wall is too high to climb over, and it is too long to walk round. Suddenly you notice a small door in the wall. It slowly opens as you watch. What do you do? Do you go through the door?
6 On the other side of the wall is water. What does it look like? Do you want to swim in it?

Interpretation

Now read about what the images represent and try to analyse your answers.

The house

The house is your idea of yourself. If your house is old, you probably do not like change, you like traditional things. If your house is large, it means you are quite confident, with a high opinion of yourself. If it is filled with light, you are optimistic. If it is dark, you are pessimistic. The number of rooms is the number of people you want in your life.

The cup

The cup is your idea of love. The more beautiful and valuable the cup, the more important love is in your life. You are a romantic person. The contents of the cup show what your experience of love has been so far.

The building

The building is your idea of religion and God. A strong building is a strong belief. A ruin would mean a lack of belief.

The garden

This is your idea of the world around you, your country, or the whole world. If the plants and flowers in your garden are dying, this might mean that you are worried about the environment and pollution in the world.

The wall

This is your idea of death. Is it the end or is there something after it? Do you go straight through the little door? Do you look and check before you go? Or don't you want to go through at all?

The water

The water is your idea of your future. If there is a sea with big waves, you feel positive and excited about your future. If you want to swim, you feel confident and want to take risks. If the water is a stagnant pool, you might fear your future and the future of the world.

● Vocabulary

Multi-word verbs

A multi-word verb is a verb + a particle (adverb or preposition).

1 Many have a literal meaning.
*The dentist **pulled out** the tooth.*
*Please **sit down** over there.*

Put one of the following words into each gap.

up	down	on	off	away
round		back		out

a. Put _____ your hat. It's cold today.
b. I don't feel well. I'm going to lie _____ for a minute.
c. I fell _____ the stairs and broke my leg.
d. The children stood _____ when the teacher arrived.
e. Don't throw _____ that bottle. We can use it again.
f. I would take _____ my jacket if I felt hot.
g. I must remember to take the book _____ to the library.
h. I'm going to take the dog _____ for a walk.
i. I heard someone running behind me. I turned _____ and saw a girl in a track suit.

2 Many multi-word verbs have a non-literal meaning.
*He's **looking after** our cat while we're on holiday.*
*The plane **took off** at six o'clock.*

Work in pairs. In the following pairs of sentences, which multi-word verb has a literal meaning, and which has a non-literal meaning? What is the non-literal meaning? Use your dictionary to help if necessary.

a. I saw 50p on the pavement and I *picked* it *up*.
I *picked up* Spanish quite quickly when I was living in Madrid.
b. *Put out* your cigarette before you go into class.
In Britain we always *put out* the milk bottles for the milkman.
c. I *looked up* the road but I couldn't see him.
She *looked up* the word in her dictionary.
d. Kate! Are you downstairs? Could you *bring up* my bag?
She *brought up* three children on her own.

3 Some multi-word verbs have an object.
*Turn off **the light**!*
*Put on **your pyjamas**.*
The particle (**off**, **on**) can change position, but if the object is a pronoun (**him**, **her**, **it**), it *must* come before the particle.
*Turn **off** the light!*
*Turn the light **off**!*
*Turn it **off**! (Not* Turn off it.)
*Put **on** your pyjamas.*
*Put your pyjamas **on**.*
*Put them **on**. (Not* Put on them.)

The sentences below can be said in three ways:

1 – as they are here
2 – with the particle in a different position
3 – with a pronoun, not a noun.

Practise the three ways.

a. I threw away his letter.
b. I took the shoes back and complained to the manager.
c. Could you look up the phone number, please?
d. Don't forget to switch the lights off.
e. Turn the radio down! It's too loud!

4 Some multi-word verbs have an object, but the particle *cannot* move.
*She **looked after** her husband while he was ill.*
*She **looked after** him.*
(*Not* She looked her husband after, or She looked him after.)

The sentences below can be said in two ways:

1 – as they are here
2 – with a pronoun, not a noun.

Practise the two ways.

a. I'm looking for my handbag.
b. Can you look after my cat?
c. I'm looking forward to the holiday.
d. John doesn't get on with his sister.

Listening and speaking

People of mixed nationality

Pre-listening task

1 What is your country? What is your nationality?
Write in the nationality adjective for the following
countries.

England   *English*   Italy   _____
France   _____   Russia   _____
Poland   _____   Malaysia   _____
China   _____   West Indies _____
Portugal _____

2 Do you have any friends or relatives who are of
mixed nationality? If so, what nationalities are their
parents or grandparents? Work with a partner and
make a list of some *advantages* and *disadvantages* that
you think might result from being of mixed
nationality.

3 **T.36a** Read and listen to the following
introduction to a radio programme about people of
mixed nationality.

'This week in *The London Programme* –
People of mixed nationality.

In the streets of London there are people
from all parts of the world. They live side
by side. Sometimes they marry and have
children. Many Londoners have parents
of a different nationality. Is this good or
bad, easy or difficult for these children?
Today two people of mixed nationality
tell us their stories.
First Amélia de Melo, a textile designer.'

Amélia de Melo
Textile designer

Listening and note-taking

T.36b Listen to the two people and take notes about
them under the headings below.
After each one, check your notes with a partner.

	Amélia	Lionel
Nationality of parents		
Languages he/ she can speak		
Advantages		
Problems		
Life now		

Lionel Varley
Architect

Comprehension check

1 Where did their parents meet?
2 Where did they live when they were children?
3 Who has visited or lived in the countries of both their
parents?
4 Why did Lionel go to Dominica? Why didn't he stay
there?
5 Why does Lionel think that he and his wife will feel
comfortable in New York?
6 What might Amélia do next summer?
7 Who are they married to?

What do you think?

1 Do you think that either Amélia or Lionel would
prefer to be of one nationality? If not, why not?
2 If you were of mixed nationality, which nationalities
would you like to be? Why?
3 Choose a country which is near to your country. How
would your life be different if you lived there?

● Everyday English

Social expressions

1 Fill the gaps in the following four short conversations with a suitable expression from the list at the side.

a. A _____ you're going to get married soon. _____ !

   B _____ , next July. July 21st. Can you come to the wedding?

   A _____ ! That's when we're away on holiday.

   B _____ , we'll send you some wedding cake.

   A That's very kind.

> That's right
> Oh, what a pity
> Congratulations
> Never mind
> I hear

b. A _____ ! Look at the time! _____ , or we'll miss the train.

   B _____ , I can't find my umbrella. Do you know where it is?

   A _____ . But you won't need it. It's a lovely day.

   B _____ . I hope you're right. Let's go.

> Hurry up
> OK
> Good heavens
> Just a minute
> I've no idea

c. A _____ in your exam!

   B _____ . I hope we both pass.

   A Did you study all last night?

   B _____ . I watched TV and went to bed early. _____ ?

   A I did the same. _____ , after the exam.

   B All right. Let's go for a drink.

> Good luck
> See you later
> Same to you
> What about you
> No, of course not

d. A I passed!

   B _____ ! I failed.

   A _____ ! What went wrong?

   B I'm always very nervous in exams, and this time I was very nervous _____ .

   A Oh, _____ . Well, all I can say is _____ .

> Bad luck
> indeed
> Well done
> I see
> better luck next time

2 ⬛ **T.37** Work in pairs. Listen and check your answers. Listen again and practise saying the dialogues together.

Present Perfect (2) – Telephoning

Giving news

PRESENTATION

1 Notice how the Present Perfect is used to express a
past action with a result in the present.

Before now   **Now**

She's cut her hair.

'I've lost my wallet.'

 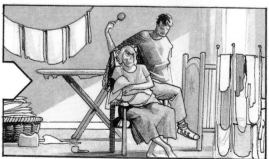

They've had a baby.

2 **T.38a** You will hear the first part of a conversation between Angela and Tom. They knew each other when they were at school together. They meet again on a London street. They haven't seen each other for a long time!

Listen and answer the questions. The verb forms in your answers are *all* Present Perfect.
a. Complete the sentences that give Angela's news.
   'I _____ to Paris.'
   'I _____ a job that I like.'
   'I _____ engaged.'
b. What has happened to Alan?
c. How do we know Angela's going to stay in Paris?
d. What news does she give about her parents?
e. In what way does Tom look different?

● **Grammar questions**

– Tom says '*I've **been** to Paris*'. Is he there now?
– Angela says '*Alan's **gone** to South America.*' Is he there now? What's the difference between **been** and **gone**?
– Did Tom finish college a long time ago?

3 What is Tom's news? Look at the pictures. What has happened to him and what has he done?

Example
He's lost weight.

PRACTICE

1 Speaking

1 Work in pairs.
   Look at the pictures. What has just happened?

2 Grammar

1 Match a line in **A** with a line in **B**.

A	B
Joe's happy because	he's just burnt the meal.
Richard's sad because	he's just had some good news.
Tim's worried because	his girlfriend's gone away on business.
Malcolm's excited because	his daughter hasn't come home yet and it's after midnight.
Ken's annoyed because	his wife's just had a baby.

2 Complete the following sentences.
  a. Mary's crying because she/just/have/some bad news.
  b. John's laughing because someone/just/tell/him a joke.
  c. My parents are furious because I/lose/the car keys.
  d. I'm fed up because someone/steal/my bike.

2 Angela and Jean-Pierre, her fiancé, are planning their wedding. Look at the list of things to do, and say what they've already done, and what they haven't done yet.

Examples
They've already booked the hotel for the reception.
They haven't ordered the cake yet.

Things to do!!
Book the hotel for the reception   ✔
Order the cake   ✘
Send out the invitations   ✘
Book the church   ✔
Decide where to go for the honeymoon   ✘
Order the flowers   ✔
Hire a suit (Jean-Pierre)   ✔
Buy a dress (Angela)   ✘
Order the champagne   ✘
Buy the wedding rings   ✔

● Language review

Present Perfect Simple

In Unit 7, we saw two uses of the Present Perfect:

1 to refer to an experience
Have you ever been to the United States?

2 to refer to an action or state which continues to the present
She's worked in a bank for five years.

In this unit we have seen another use:

3 to express a past action with a result in the present.
I've lost my wallet.

Translate

I've lost my wallet. Have you seen it?

_____

I lost it yesterday.

_____

She's already bought a ring.

_____

▶ **Grammar reference: page 131.**

PRESENTATION

1 [T.38b] Read and listen to the second part of the conversation between Angela and Tom.

Tom	Well, I've just finished college. I've been studying archaeology. And for the last month I've been working as a postman.
Angela	And what are you doing in London?
Tom	I'm trying to find a job. I've been going round museums to see if they need anybody. I've been writing letters for weeks!
Angela	Have you had many replies?
Tom	Well, a few, but not many. I've written at least thirty letters.
Angela	Poor old you! Look, let's go and have a cup of tea, and we can catch up on some more news.
Tom	What a lovely idea!

2 Complete the sentences about Tom.

 a. He's *been studying* archaeology.

 b. He _____ as a postman.

 c. He _____ museums looking for a job.

 d. He _____ letters for weeks.

 e. He _____ at least thirty letters.

● Grammar questions

– Sentences **a.–e.** have examples of the Present Perfect. Are they Simple or Continuous?
– Look at sentences **d.** and **e.**
 Which is more interested in the *activity* of writing?
 Which is more interested in the *quantity* of writing?

● Language review

Present Perfect Continuous

The Present Perfect Continuous has two uses which are similar to the Present Perfect Simple form:

1 to refer to an activity which continues to the present
 I've been learning English for three years.
 If the verb expresses a state (not an activity), the simple form must be used.
 I've had this book for six months.

2 to refer to an activity with a result in the present
 I'm tired because I've been working hard.

Translate

Angela lives in Paris.

_____

She's been living in Paris for a year.

_____

I've known Tom for years.

_____

I'm hot because I've been running.

_____

▶ **Grammar reference: page 131.**

PRACTICE

1 Grammar

1 Choose the correct verb form.
 a. How long *has Angela been living/does Angela live* in Paris?
 b. She *has been finding/has found* a good job.
 c. Alan *has been/has gone* to South America.
 d. Angela *has bought/bought* her flat a few months ago.
 e. How long *has she known/has she been knowing* Jean-Pierre?
 f. Tom *worked/has been working* as a postman for a month.
 g. He *has visited/has been visiting* ten museums today.
 h. He's tired because he *has travelled/has been travelling* around London all day.

2 Put the verbs in brackets in the correct tense, Present Perfect or Past Simple. If both the Present Perfect Simple and Continuous are possible, use the Continuous.

 a. How long _____ you _____ (learn) English?

 b. How long _____ you _____ (use) this book?

 c. Which book _____ you _____ (have) before this one?

 d. How long _____ you _____ (know) your teacher?

 e. How long _____ you _____ (play) tennis/football?

 f. When _____ you _____ (start) playing?

 Now answer the questions about you!

2 Speaking

Look at the pictures. Make a sentence about the people, using an idea from the box. Then add **because** and say what they've been doing.

Example
1 *He's hot because he's been running.*

hot	wet	back hurts	red cheeks
dirty hands	tired	eyes hurt	
no money	paint on her clothes		

SKILLS DEVELOPMENT

● Reading and speaking

Pre-reading task

1 In groups, discuss the following questions.

– Do you like flying?
 If you do, what do you like best about it?
 If you don't, what do you dislike most?

– 'Flying used to be exciting and glamorous, but not any more' – do you agree?

– 'Flying is tiring because you are so passive. You have no control over what you do' – do you agree?

– Do you like airports?
 Which is your favourite airport?

2 Read the definitions of the following words.

wellington boots (*n*)	long rubber boots, e.g. for gardening
a cockpit (*n*)	the part of a plane where the pilot sits
to smudge (*v*)	to make something messy, e.g. 'I won't give you a kiss because I don't want to smudge my lipstick.'
deserted (*adj*)	empty, with no people
a runway (*n*)	the long, straight 'road' at an airport where planes take off and land
mist (*n*)	cloud of tiny drops of water in the air, e.g. early morning mists in autumn
par excellence (*id*)	a French term, which means 'better than anything else like it', e.g. a writer *par excellence*

Reading

You will now read an extract from a book called *Airport International*. It is about the beginning of air travel and its growth over the years. (The extract mentions Southend, which is a town on the south-east coast of England.) Read the text. Fill each gap with one of the following verb forms.

approaching	seen	grown	operating
jammed	built	tops	become
	shares	jumped	

Flying – then and now

1 My first flight was from Paris to Portsmouth in 1959. The pilot arrived late, with the stewardess. He wore a leather coat, old trousers, and wellington boots. The stewardess had holes in her stockings and wore mirrored sunglasses. They both went into the cockpit without a word.

2 When we were (a)_____ the English coast, the stewardess appeared in the cabin. She was still wearing the sunglasses, but her lipstick was smudged. 'Southend? Anyone for Southend?' she shouted. The boy in front of me put up his hand. The DC3 suddenly landed. The boy was shown the door and he (b)_____ down onto the grass field, and we took off again. The stewardess went back into the cockpit. I remember thinking at the time that flying wouldn't always be like this.

3 And I was right. In 30 years, international travel has completely changed, and the world has (c)_____ a global village. Crossing the world is as easy as (sometimes easier than) getting from one side of a city to another. The world of air travel has developed into a huge industry.

4 The airports themselves are remarkable places: Paris's strange and space-like Charles de Gaulle, or Dallas/Fort Worth with its Texan vastness. There are airports which are almost (d)_____ with the number of arrivals and departures, like Chicago's O'Hare or Tokyo's Haneda; and there are deserted airports like Tanzania's Kilimanjaro, lying beneath the snows of that great mountain, waiting for the tourists who have never arrived.

5 But probably one of the greatest of them all is London's Heathrow, which (e)_____ the list of both international flights and international passengers. In 1989, it handled 355,000 flights and over 38 million passengers with 57 million items of luggage. It has (f)_____ into a city in its own right, employing 53,000 people full time.

Like all the great airports, it dates back only to the last days of the Second World War.

6 The first runway was (g)_____ on the flat land near the village of Staines in 1944. It was a place of historic interest. One of the most important Anglo-Saxon temples is buried under Terminal Two, and the village of Heathrow is now under the main car park. The airport has ghosts. A Saxon prince has been (h)_____ near the ponds, where he drowned, and an outlaw rides through the cargo sheds, with a three-cornered hat and a black horse. Heathrow has been (i)_____ as an international airport since 1 January 1946, when a British South American Airways Lancastrian took off into the morning mists on a flight to Buenos Aires. In February 1952, the Queen arrived from Entebbe to set foot on British soil for the first time as monarch.

7 Since those early days, constant building has been necessary to deal with the growth of air traffic and the demands of air travellers. However, Heathrow (j)_____ the same problems as all big airports – too many planes, too many people, and too much crime. It is the centre-point of the great air routes between Europe and North America in one direction, and between Europe and the Gulf, Africa, and Asia in the other. It is alive with all the citizens of this strange world, rich and poor, honest and dishonest. It is the Airport International *par excellence*.

(Adapted from *Airport International*, by Brian Moynahan)

Comprehension check

1 Here are summaries of the seven paragraphs. Match them to the correct paragraph.
  a. _____ Heathrow, one of the world's biggest airports
  b. _____ The growth of international travel
  c. _____ An unusual stopover
  d. _____ Some airports around the world
  e. _____ The crew on an early flight
  f. _____ Heathrow, its growth and its problems
  g. _____ The history of Heathrow

2 What point is the writer making in the first two paragraphs?

3 What do the crew usually do during a flight today? In what way was the writer's first experience of flying different from the routines of today?

4 What do you understand by the term 'global village'?

5 What are some of the facts that make Heathrow a remarkable airport?

6 What do you understand by the following line from paragraph 7 '(Heathrow) is alive with all the citizens of this strange world . . .'?

7 Read this summary of the text. There are some mistakes in it. Say if the sentences are true or false.

> The writer took a plane for the first time in 1959.
>
> He was impressed by the crew's uniforms.
>
> The pilot and stewardess worked together in the cockpit.
>
> The stewardess hadn't put her make-up on properly.
>
> The plane suddenly stopped to let a boy off.
>
> Since then, air travel has developed and improved.
>
> It has become easy to fly all over the world.
>
> O'Hare, Haneda, and Kilimanjaro are busy airports.
>
> Heathrow has more international flights than any other airport.
>
> It was built in 1944.
>
> The first international flight from Heathrow was to Argentina.
>
> Heathrow has become successful because of its geographical position.
>
> It has problems because it isn't big enough.

Vocabulary

Word families and word stress

1 The words below have all appeared in the previous four units of *Headway Pre-Intermediate*.
Put them in the correct row according to their stress pattern.

discovery   invention   disappearance
discussion   computer   advertisement
celebration   argument   development
authority   government   accommodation
existence   behaviour

1 ●●●	
2 ●●●	
3 ●●●●	
4 ●●●●	*discovery*
5 ●●●●●	

2 The words in exercise **1** are all nouns.
What are the verbs? Be careful with word stress!

3 Put the following words into the correct row according to their stress pattern.

generous   determined   valuable
reliable   comfortable   scientific
technological

1 ●●●●	
2 ●●●●	
3 ●●●	
4 ●●●	
5 ●●●●	

4 The words in exercise **3** are all adjectives. What are the nouns? Be careful with word stress.

5 Fill the gaps by adding a suffix to the word in brackets.
 a. My father's very _____ (act) even though he's seventy.
 b. I've always wanted to work in the theatre, but _____ (act) isn't a very secure profession.
 c. _____ (Hope), we'll soon find a solution to the problem.
 d. Look _____ (care) left and right before crossing the road.
 e. It was very _____ (care) of you to lose my watch.
 f. I take two _____ (day) newspapers and three Sunday papers.
 g. You've broken my camera! Look at it! It's _____ (use)!
 h. Thanks for the advice. It was really _____ (use).
 i. I have some very _____ (noise) neighbours.
 j. She became _____ (fame) as a result of her invention.

Listening and speaking

Phoning home
When young people in Britain go to college or university, they often go to another part of the country. They don't usually stay at home.
Justin is twenty, and is studying away from home in the north of England. He never writes home, but often rings his parents on Sunday evening.

108

Listening

1 **T.39a** Listen to Justin's side of the conversation, and say whether the following statements are true or false.

a. Justin has been working hard for his exams.
b. His first exam was last Tuesday.
c. He wants to tell his mother about the exam.
d. Justin's mother has not heard about Lucinda before.
e. Justin and Lucinda have been getting ready for tomorrow's exam.
f. Lucinda is studying Chinese.
g. Justin's mother has been getting ready to go to Geneva.
h. Justin's father usually works in the garden on Sundays.
i. Term ends on the thirtieth.
j. Justin asks his mother a favour.

2 Work in pairs.
Listen to Justin again. Your teacher will stop the tape. What do you think his mother said?

3 **T.39b** Now listen to both sides of the conversation. Compare what she says with your ideas.

Roleplay
Work in pairs. Imagine it is last Sunday evening. One of you phones the other for a chat. Ask and answer about what you've been doing over the weekend.

● **Everyday English**

Telephoning

1 Practise saying the following telephone numbers.
071 927 4863   09278 4098   633488
061 44 501277
What is *your* phone number?

2 **T.40** You will hear three telephone conversations. Listen, and for each one say:
 – who is speaking to who
 – what about
 – how well they know each other.

3 Notice the following expressions:
  52902 (*Not* Here is 52902, or This is 52902)
  This is John. (*Not* Here is John, or I'm John.)
  Could I speak to Ann Baker, please? (*Not* speak with.)
  Is that Mike?
  I'm afraid he's out.
  Can I take a message?
  I'll try again later.
 What do the following mean?
  Hold on. I'll connect you.
  Speaking.
 Ask your teacher for tapescript **40**. Practise saying the conversations.

4 Your teacher will give you a role card.
Prepare what you are going to say, and then be ready to make a call or answer the phone.

Past Perfect – Reported statements and questions

All you need is love

PRESENTATION

1 The following are summaries of a magazine story called *Hot Lips* by Celia Young. Read and compare the two versions, **A** and **B**.

The story so far. . .

A Marsha met Felix at a party one Saturday night. They fell passionately in love and got married the following Saturday. After the wedding, Felix moved into Marsha's flat. Marsha phoned her parents and told them her news. They were surprised and angry. Unfortunately, after a few months, Felix met another woman and his marriage to Marsha started to go wrong . . .

B Marsha and Felix got married one Saturday in June. They had met only one week earlier at a party and had fallen passionately in love. Marsha rang and told her parents her news after the wedding, when Felix had moved into her flat. They were surprised and angry. Unfortunately, after a few months, their marriage started to go wrong. Felix had met another woman . . .

2 In version **A**, the events of the story are given in chronological order. Put into the brackets under **B** the order in which the same events are given in version **B**. Two have been done for you.

	A	B	
Marsha and Felix met.	(1)	(2)	*had met*
They fell in love.	(2)	( )	
They got married.	(3)	(1)	*got married*
Felix moved into Marsha's flat.	(4)	( )	
Marsha told her parents.	(5)	( )	
They were angry.	(6)	( )	
Felix met another woman.	(7)	( )	
The marriage started to go wrong.	(8)	( )	

3 Write the verb forms from version **B** on the lines in exercise **2**. Two have been done for you. Practise saying the sentences.

> They'd met at a party.
> They'd fallen passionately in love.

4 Are the following statements about Marsha and Felix true or false? If they are false, correct them.
   a. Marsha and Felix hadn't known each other very long when they got married.
   b. When Marsha told her parents about the wedding, Felix hadn't moved into her flat.
   c. Her parents were angry because she hadn't told them about the wedding.
   d. The marriage started to go wrong, and then Felix met another woman.

● Grammar questions

– What tense are all the verb forms in version **A**?
– 'Verb forms in the Past Simple tell a story in chronological order.'
   Is this true or false?
– Text **B** contains examples of the Past Perfect. Complete this rule:
   The Past Perfect is formed with the auxiliary verb _____ + the _____ _____ .
– What does the Past Perfect express?

PRACTICE

1 Speaking

1 The story is continued in the pictures.
Work in pairs. First tell the story in the order of the pictures.

Then tell the story again, but begin at picture **4**.
   When Marsha arrived home, Felix . . .

2 Make sentences from the chart below.

1

Felix . . . his suitcase.

Then he . . .

3

and . . .

Marsha . . . home.

I My teacher My leg The plants The house	was in a mess was late for work was hungry died was angry hurt went to bed early apologized	because	I we my alarm clock	had hadn't	fallen over playing tennis. gone off. had a busy day. done the homework. forgotten to water them. tidied up after the party. been rude the day before. had any breakfast.

2 Grammar

Work in pairs.
Look at the verb forms in these sentences.
What is the difference in meaning between them?

a. When Marsha arrived home, Felix *was packing/
packed/had packed* his suitcase.

b. The concert *started/had started* when we arrived.

c. When the police arrived, the robber *climbed/had
climbed/was climbing* out of the window.

3 Listening and pronunciation

The **had** in the Past Perfect tense is often contracted.
   I'd locked the door, but I hadn't closed the window.
The **'d** is sometimes difficult to hear.
'd is also the contracted form of **would**:
   I'd like to come.

T.41   Listen to the sentences. Put a tick if the
sentence contains an example of the Past Perfect.

a. _____   c. _____   e. _____   g. _____   i. _____

b. _____   d. _____   f. _____   h. _____   j. _____

4 Reading and grammar

Put the verbs in brackets into the correct tense, Past
Simple or Past Perfect.

The end of the story

Marsha (a)_____ (read) Felix's letter and
then she (b)_____ (walk) slowly into the
kitchen.

She (c)_____ (buy) his favourite food for
dinner. She (d)_____ (throw) it in the rubbish
bin. Why (e)_____ he (f)_____ (do) this to
her? She remembered how happy they
(g)_____ (be) in the beginning. They
(h)_____ (laugh) a lot then. Marsha (i)_____
(feel) desperate.

One hour later the phone (j)_____ (ring) in
the flat. It was Marsha's parents, but she
(k)_____ (not answer) the phone. She . . .

Now finish the story!

112

● Language review

Past Perfect

The Past Perfect is used to make clear that one past
action happened before another past action.

Translate

When I arrived, she had left.

_____

When I arrived, she left.

_____

▶ **Grammar reference: page 131.**

PRESENTATION

Study the following charts of direct and reported
speech.

1 Write the names of the tenses of the verbs in italics in
the spaces beneath.

Direct statements	Reported statements
I often *play* tennis. _Present Simple_	She said (that) she often *played* tennis. _____
She's *staying* with her aunt. _____	He said (that) she *was staying* with her aunt. _____
She *went* to Moscow alone. _____	He said (that) she *had gone* to Moscow alone. _____
He's *gone* home. _____	She said (that) he *had gone* home. _____
I'll *go* with Anna. _____	He said (that) he *would go* with Anna. _Past of will_

● Grammar questions

- What tense change takes place from direct to reported speech?
- Which two tenses in direct speech change to the *same* tense in reported speech?
2 Now study the chart on direct and reported questions. When you have answered the grammar questions below, try to complete the chart.

	Direct questions	Reported questions
	Where's John?	He asked where John was.
	How many cigarettes do you smoke?	She asked how many cigarettes I smoked.
	Why did Anna go to Moscow?	He asked why Anna had gone to Moscow.
	Have you seen Jim?	He asked if I had seen Jim.
	Do you like whisky?	_____
	Why are you laughing?	_____
	Where has John gone?	_____
	Who did Anna meet?	_____

● Grammar questions

- How is the punctuation different in direct and reported questions?
- What changes in word order are there?
- What word is used in reported questions when there is no question word in the direct question?

PRACTICE

1 Grammar

Report the following statements and questions.
a. 'I love Anna,' said Jim.
b. 'Do you love me, Jim?' Anna asked.
c. 'I'm leaving on Sunday,' she said.
d. 'Where are you going?' he asked her.
e. 'Mr Walker phoned before lunch, but he didn't leave a message,' Sue said.
f. 'Have there been any messages for me?' Miss Wilson asked.
g. 'I don't think it'll rain,' he said.
h. 'Why didn't you tell Anna the truth?' Mary asked Jim.

2 Speaking

Work in pairs.
1 Read the following report of an interview with Celia Young, the writer of *Hot Lips*.

I asked Celia Young why she had written another romantic novel. She said that she found romantic fiction easy to write, but that her next novel wouldn't be a romance. She was hoping to write something different, possibly a detective story.

I told her that I was interested in the character of Felix, and I asked if he was anyone she knew from real life. Celia laughed and replied that she was glad that she didn't have a Felix in her life, and that she had been happily married for over fifteen years to Richard Marsh, the politician. I said that she had now written five novels, and I asked when she had started writing. She answered that she had written stories and poems all her life and that she would continue to write even when she was an old lady.

I thanked her for talking to me and said that I hoped that *Hot Lips* would be successful.

2 On a separate piece of paper, write the actual words of the interview in direct speech. The beginning has been done for you.

Interviewer   Why have you written another romantic novel?
Celia Young   I find romantic fiction easy to write, but my next novel won't be a romance. I'm hoping to . . .

3 **T.42** Now listen to the interview, and compare it with yours.

113

Reported statements

The usual rule in reported statements is that the verb form moves one tense back.

'I'm leaving.' *He said (that) he was leaving.*
'She went home early.' *He said (that) she'd (had) gone home early.*
'She's gone.' *He said (that) she'd gone.*

Notice that the Past Simple and the Present Perfect both change to the Past Perfect.

Translate

He said he was leaving.

_____

She told me that he had gone home.

_____

Reported questions

In reported questions the word order is not the same as in direct questions.

'Where are you going?' *He asked me where I was going.*

As in reported statements the usual rule is one tense back. When there is no question word, **if** is used in reported questions.

Translate

She asked me if I had seen John.

_____

▶ **Grammar reference: page 131.**

SKILLS DEVELOPMENT

● Reading and speaking

You are going to read a parable written in the nineteenth century. A parable is a short story about everyday things which is told to make a moral or religious point.

Pre-reading task

1 Work in groups. Tell each other some parables (perhaps religious stories), or some fables (for example, Aesop's fables). What is the moral of the story?

2 Check that you understand the title of the story.
If you could turn back the clock, think of some things you could do.

Examples
If you lost a point at tennis, you could play the point again until you won.
You could win a lot of money on the football pools, because you would know the results.

Reading
Read the story up to line 30, and answer the questions. Don't worry about any words you don't know.

THE MAN WHO COULD TURN BACK THE CLOCK

THIS IS A PARABLE WITH TWO DIFFERENT ENDINGS. READERS CAN CHOOSE THE ENDING THEY LIKE BEST.

ONCE upon a time there was a man who had the power to turn back the clock. Whenever he regretted something he had done or said, he could repeat the event in the light of experience.

5 Now one day it happened that this man was out for a walk when it started to rain, so he took shelter in a barn. After a few minutes the man was joined by a very beautiful young lady and her dog, who were also seeking shelter. The downpour lasted
10 about an hour.

The man went home to his wife and told her why he was late. Immediately his wife was suspicious of her husband's behaviour with the young lady. She questioned him about what had happened. The
15 man replied in a surprised and hurt voice: 'Why, nothing happened. I was a perfect gentleman. What do you expect? Especially when she had such a large dog with her.'

His wife was furious: 'What!! Only the dog
20 stopped you!'

The man realized his mistake and immediately he turned the clock back a few minutes and tried

the conversation again. This time when his wife expressed her suspicion, he said 'It's true the girl
25 was very beautiful and she seemed to like me but my deep love for you gave me the strength to resist temptation.'

However, his wife was even more furious: 'What!! You wanted to kiss her! An immoral thought is as
30 bad as an immoral deed.'

1

The man spent a long time thinking. There must be some way to please his wife!
35 Finally he turned the clock back again a few minutes. Once more his wife asked how he had behaved with the beau-
40 tiful young lady. But this time he replied: 'What? She wasn't beautiful, she was ugly! I am a man with good
45 taste, which is why I married you, my darling!'

When she heard this, his wife, who in fact was rather unattractive,
50 flung her arms around his neck and cried, 'I love you!'

2

The man felt that his wonderful power had
55 not helped him at all. Except to teach him that it was impossible to please his wife, and he had suspected this
60 for a long time. Therefore he turned back the clock once more, not just a few minutes, but a few hours. He went
65 back to the beautiful young lady in the barn, in the rain.

ADAPTED FROM A STORY
BY RALPH MILNE FARLEY.

Comprehension check
1 How many times did the man turn back the clock?
2 What mistakes had he made?
3 How did his wife react?

Work in pairs. In the story, two possible endings are given. Before you read them, work out an ending. What would you do if you were the man with the power? Now read the two endings. Is either of them like yours?

What do you think?
1 Which ending do you prefer? Why?
2 What are the morals of the different endings?

Vocabulary
It is often possible to guess the meaning of words you don't know by looking at the context.

Example
l.6 took shelter
took is a verb, and **shelter** is probably a noun. When it starts to rain, people don't want to get wet, they want to escape from the rain. So maybe *took shelter* means *escaped from.*

Try to guess the meaning of the following words.
l.3 regretted
l.4 in the light of experience
l.7 a barn
l.9 seeking
l.9 the downpour
l.12 suspicious
l.15 hurt
l.26 to resist temptation
l.30 an immoral deed
l.50 flung

Vocabulary

Bring/take and come/go

1 The choice between **bring** and **take** and **come** and **go** depends on where the speaker is. **Bring** and **come** are used for a movement towards the speaker. **Take** and **go** are used for a movement away from the speaker.

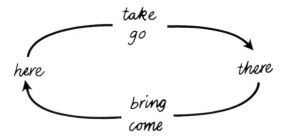

2 Fill the gaps with a suitable form of one of the four verbs.
  a. 'Goodbye everyone! I'm _____ on holiday.'
  'Where are you _____?'
  'To Australia. I'm _____ my family to visit the Great Barrier Reef.'
  'Have a good time! When you _____ back, _____ me a T-shirt!'
  'OK!'
  b. (Teacher to class)
  'Remember to _____ your dictionary to class tomorrow, and prepare the dialogues. We're _____ to the language laboratory at 10.00.'
  c. (Conversation at home)
  'What time did you _____ home last night? I didn't hear you.'
  'It was after midnight. Mike _____ me home in his car.'
  d. (Someone on the phone)
  'You must _____ and see my new flat. It's beautiful. And _____ Jane, too. She'll love it.'
  e. (Swiss student talking in England)
  'When I _____ home to Switzerland, I'm going to _____ a jumper for my mother and some whisky for my father.'
  f. (Spanish student talking in Spain)
  'I'm _____ to London in a few days, so tonight we're having a little party at home. Some friends are _____ round, and we'll have something to eat. They're _____ some things that they want me to _____ to London, because they have friends there and want to give them a present.'

Get

Get is one of the most common verbs in spoken English, but it is not used so much in written English. **Get** can suggest a change of some sort.
  The weather is getting colder.
  I got dressed and went to work.

He's fine.   He's getting tired.   He's tired.

She's ill.   She's getting better.   She's better.

Notice how the verb **to be** is used to show the completed change, and **get** to show the process of changing.
  *I **am** married.*
  *I **got married** ten years ago.*
  *Where did you **get married**?*

Fill the gaps with a form of **get** and one of the words in the box.

worried	difficult	late	divorced
wet	married	ready	angry	lost

a. We were having a lovely walk, but then it started to rain and we _____ _____ .
b. Jenny and Bob are in love. They are _____ _____ next spring. I hope they'll be very happy.
c. 'What happened to Tom and Barbara? Are they still together?'
'No, they _____ _____ .'
d. I _____ very _____ when my children break their toys and expect me to buy new ones.
e. The traffic in town is awful. It's _____ more and more _____ to drive anywhere, and it's impossible to park.
f. Come on! We'd better go. It's _____ _____ .
g. How long does it take you to _____ _____ in the morning?
h. Make sure you phone me regularly. I _____ _____ when I don't hear from you.
i. Sorry we're late. We _____ _____ on the way here.

Listening and writing

A love song

Pre-listening task

You are going to listen to one of Elvis Presley's songs.
It is called *The Girl of My Best Friend*.
Work in pairs.

1 What do you think the song is about?
2 Look at the words in the box below. Which of them rhyme?

arms	forever	mend	rain
bad	friend	miss	sad
broken heart	hair	moon	talks
end	hold	never	tears
eyes	June	pain	tell
face	kiss	part	together
fair	leave	place	walks
fears	lies	pretend	weather

3 Choose at least eight of the words and write a poem about someone you love. The problem is that you haven't told him/her! The rhymes will help you.
4 Read your poem to the rest of the class.

Listening

1 Look at the words of the song.
Try to put a word from the box in exercise **2** into each gap.

2 **T.43** Listen to the song. Check that the words you wrote in the gaps are the same as in the song.

The girl of my best friend

The way she _____,
The way she _____,
How long can I _____?
Oh I can't help it, I'm in love
With the girl of my best friend.

Her lovely _____,
Her skin so _____,
I could go on and never _____.
Oh I can't help it, I'm in love
With the girl of my best friend.

I want to _____ her how I love her so,
And _____ her in my _____, but then
What if she got real mad and told him so?
I could never _____ either one again.

The way they _____,
Their happiness;
Will my aching heart ever _____?
Or will I always be in love
With the girl of my best friend?

3 Now listen and sing the song!

117

● Everyday English

Saying goodbye

1 All the people in the following pictures are saying goodbye to each other, but the captions have been mixed up. Put the correct caption with each picture.

a. 'Goodbye! Drive carefully and call us when you get there!'	**b.** 'Bye! See you later. Are you doing anything tonight?'	**c.** 'Goodbye! Have a safe journey. Send us a postcard!'	**d.** 'Goodbye. Here's my number. Please get in touch if you have any problems with it.'
e. 'Goodbye. It's been most interesting talking to you. We'll let you know by post.'	**f.** 'Goodbye! Good luck in the future. I've really enjoyed our lessons together!'	**g.** 'Bye-bye! Thank you very much for having me.'	**h.** 'Goodbye. Thank you for a lovely evening. You must come to us next time.'

2 **T.44** Listen to the sentences, and practise saying them.

Now do the Stop and Check on page 78 of the Workbook.

Jigsaw activities

Unit 2 page 14 **Student B**

NAME AND AGE	TOWN AND COUNTRY	FAMILY	OCCUPATION	FREE TIME / HOLIDAY	PRESENT ACTIVITY
MIGUEL 26	- Palma / Majorca - Spain	- not married - 2 older brothers	- barman in his parents' hotel	- sailing - London every autumn to learn English	- staying with his brother in Madrid
CHANTAL 34	- Paris - France	- not married - 3 sisters - 2 brothers	- fashion buyer	- Moroccan restaurants - jogging - holiday home in Biarritz	- buying clothes in New York
EMMA 15					
MARIO and RITA CUMINO 65 and 63					

Unit 9 page 70

Information for Student A (Exercise 4)
You work in a railway ticket office.
Give **Student B** the information he/she wants.

Trains to Bristol

Depart		Arrive
11.25	change at Reading	12.35
11.50	direct	12.50

Tickets
Single	£13.50
Day return	£19.00
Period return	£22.40

Information for Student B (Exercise 5)
You work in a railway ticket office.
Give **Student A** the information he/she wants.

Trains to Manchester

Depart		Arrive
11.05	change at Derby	13.30
12.05	change at Derby	14.30

Tickets
Single	£19.00
Day return	£27.60
Period return	£36.20

Unit 10 page 73 **Student B**

A Love Story

George loves Lily.
George phones Lily _____. (How often?)
He sends her flowers every week.
George wrote a _____ for Lily.
The poem was about her blue eyes and red lips.
One day George saw Lily in the _____. (Where?)
She was talking to James.
_____ gave Lily some flowers.
James kissed Lily.
Suddenly Lily saw _____.
George hit James.
_____ saw George.
The policeman took George to the police station.
_____ drove Lily home.
Lily got married to James.
George wrote a _____.
It was called 'Death in the Park'.

Grammar section

UNIT 1

Question forms

1 Questions with question words
Questions can begin with a question
word.

what   where   which   how
who   when   why   whose

'**Where**'s the station?'
  'In Baker Street.'
'**Why** are you laughing?'
  'Because you look funny.'
'**Whose** is this coat?'
  'Mine.'
'**How** does she go to work?'
  'By train.'

Note
1 What, which, and **whose** can be
followed by a noun.
What size do you take?
Which coat is yours?
Whose book is this?

2 Which is generally used when there
is a limited choice.
Which is your husband? The blond
one or the dark one?
This rule is not always true!

What
Which | newspaper do you read?

3 How can be followed by an
adjective or an adverb.
How big is his new car?
How fast does it go?

---

2 Questions with no question word
The answer to these questions is **yes** or
no.
'Are you hot?'
  '**Yes, I am**.'/'**No, I'm not**.'
'Is she working?'
  '**Yes, she is**.'/'**No, she isn't**.'
'Does he smoke?'
  '**Yes, he does**.'/'**No, he doesn't**.'
'Can you swim?'
  '**Yes, I can**.'/'**No, I can't**.'

▶ **Form**

1 Verb forms with an auxiliary verb

Positive   *She is reading.*

Question   *Is she reading?*

Positive   *They are watching a film.*

Question   *What are they watching?*

Positive   *She can drive.*

Question   *Can she drive?*

2 Verb forms with no auxiliary verb
In the Present Simple and the Past
Simple, there is no auxiliary verb in the
positive.
*They **live** in London.*
*He **arrived** yesterday.*

Do/does/did is used in the question.
***Do** they live in London?*
*Where **does** Bill come from?*
*When **did** he arrive?*

Present Continuous

▶ **Form**

am
is | + verb + **-ing** (present participle)
are

Positive and negative

I	'm (am) 'm not	
He She It	's (is) isn't	working.
We You They	're (are) aren't	

Question

	am	I	
What	is	he she it	wearing?
	are	we you they	

Short answer
'**Are** you going?'
'Yes, I **am**.'/'No, I'm **not**.'

'**Is** Anna working?'
'Yes, she **is**.'/'No, she **isn't**.'

Note
We cannot use **I'm**, **we're**, **she's**, etc. in
short answers.
Wrong Yes, I'm.
           Yes, she's.
Right   Yes, I **am**.
          Yes, she **is**.

▶ **Use**

The Present Continuous is used
1 to express an activity happening now.
   *They're **playing** football in the garden.*
   She can't answer the phone because she's
   ***washing** her hair.*

2 to express an activity happening around
   now, but perhaps not at the moment of
   speaking.
   *She's **studying** Maths at university.*
   *I'm **reading** a good book by Henry*
   James.

3 to express a planned future
   arrangement.
   *I'm **meeting** Miss Boyd at ten o'clock*
   tomorrow.
   *He's **starting** French lessons next week.*
   *What **are** you **doing** at the weekend?*

UNIT 2

Present Simple

▶ Form

Positive and negative

I We You They	live don't live	
He She It	lives doesn't live	near here.

Question

Where do	I we you they	live?
Where does	he she it	

Short answer

'*Do you like Peter?*'
'*Yes, I do.*'
'*Does she speak French?*'
'*No, she doesn't.*'

▶ Use

The Present Simple is used
1 to express a habit.
   I get up at 7.30.
   Dutch people travel a lot.
2 to express a fact which is always true.
   Vegetarians don't eat meat.
   We come from Spain.
3 to express a fact which is true for a long time.
   I live in Oxford.
   She works in a bank.

Present Simple and Present Continuous

1 Look at the use of the Present Simple and the Present Continuous in the following sentences.

   Do you wear a uniform at work?
   Why are you wearing that funny hat?

   I watch TV nearly every night.
   Sh! I'm watching a good film!

   Annie works in an office.
   It's Sunday now. She isn't working.
   She's reading at home.

2 Look at the wrong sentences, and compare them with the right sentences.

×	Where is she coming from?
√	Where does she come from?
×	Are you liking Coke?
√	Do you like Coke?
×	Who do you speak to on the telephone?
√	Who are you speaking to on the telephone?
×	I read a good book at the moment.
√	I'm reading a good book at the moment.

Have/have got

▶ Form

Positive

I We You They	have 've got	two sisters.
He She	has 's got	

Negative

I We You They	don't have haven't got	
He She	doesn't have hasn't got	any money.

Question

Do	I we you they	have a car?
Does	he she	

Have	I we you they	got a car?
Has	he she	

Short answer

'*Have you got a camera?*'
'*Yes, I have.*/'*No, I haven't.*'

'*Do you have a camera?*'
'*Yes, I do.*'/'*No, I don't.*'

> **Note**
> We can use the contractions ('**ve** and '**s**) with **have got**, but not with **have**.
> *I've got a sister.*
> *I have a sister.*
> **Wrong** *I've a sister.*

▶ Use

1 **Have** and **have got** mean the same. **Have got** is informal. We use it a lot when we speak, but not when we write.
   '*Have you got a light?*'
   The Prime Minister has a meeting with the President today.
2 **Have** and **have got** express possession.
   I've got
   I have a new car.

   She's got
   She has three children.

   He's got
   He has blond hair.

When **have** + noun means an activity or a habit, **have** and the **do/does/don't/doesn't** forms are used. **Have got** is not used.

I have lunch at 1.00.

Look at the wrong sentences and compare them with the right sentences.

×	I've got a shower in the morning.
√	I have a shower in the morning.
×	What time have you got lunch?
√	What time do you have lunch?
×	He has never got milk in his coffee.
√	He never has milk in his coffee.

> **Note**
> In the past tense, the **got** forms are unusual. **Had** with **did** and **didn't** is much more common.
> *I had a bicycle when I was young.*
> *My parents had a lot of books in the house.*
> *Did you have a nice weekend?*
> *I didn't have any money when I was a student.*

UNIT 3

Past Simple

▶ Form

The form of the Past Simple is the same for all persons.

Positive

The positive of regular verbs ends in **-ed**. There are many common irregular verbs. See the list on page 141.

I He/She/It We You They	finished arrived went	yesterday.

Negative

The negative of the Past Simple is formed with **didn't**.

He walk ed.

He didn't walk .

I She You etc.	didn't (did not)	arrive yesterday.

Question

The question in the Past Simple is formed with **did**.

She finish ed.

When did she finish ?

When did	she you they etc.	arrive?

Short answer

'*Did you go to work yesterday?*'
'*Yes, I did.*'

'*Did it rain last night?*'
'*No, it didn't.*'

▶ Use

The Past Simple is used

1 to express a finished action in the past.
We played tennis last Sunday.
I worked in London from 1984 to 1989.
John left two minutes ago.

> **Note**
> The Past Simple is often used with past time expressions: *last year, last month, five years ago, yesterday morning, in 1945.*

2 to express actions which follow each other in a story.

James came into the room. He took off his coat and sat down on the bed. Suddenly, he noticed somebody behind the curtain. He stood up and walked slowly across the room . . .

Past Continuous

▶ Form

was/were (past tense of **to be**) + verb + **-ing** (present participle)

Positive and negative

I He She It	was wasn't (was not)	working.
We You They	were weren't (were not)	

Question

What	was	I he she it	doing?
	were	we you they	

Short answer

'*Were you working yesterday?*'
'*Yes, I was.*'

'*Was she studying when you arrived?*'
'*No, she wasn't.*'

▶ Use

The Past Continuous is used to express a past activity happening over a period of time.

Last night 8 p.m. 9 p.m. 10 p.m. Now

| – – – – – – – – – – |
watching TV

'*What were you doing at 9.00 last night?*'
'*I was watching TV.*' (I started watching before 9.00, and continued after 9.00.)

Past Simple and Past Continuous

Look at the use of the Past Continuous and the Past Simple in the following sentences.

I was doing my homework at 7.00 last night. (I was in the middle of the activity.)
I did my homework last night. (I started and finished.)

I was doing my homework when Jack arrived.
When the teacher arrived, the students were talking.
(*Doing my homework* and *talking* are long activities. Something happened in the middle to interrupt them.)

The teacher arrived. Then they started the lesson. (Here, there are two activities, one followed by another.)

The moon was shining through the window. James Bond came into the room and sat down on the bed. (In stories, the Past Continuous is often used to describe the scene. The Past Simple tells the action.)

UNIT 4

Expressions of quantity

some/any   much/many   a lot of/lots of
a few/a little

▶ **Use**

To use expressions of quantity correctly, you need to understand the difference between countable and uncountable nouns.

Countable nouns	Uncountable nouns
a cup	water
a girl	sugar
an apple	milk
an egg	music
a guitar	weather
a pound	money

We can say **three cups, two girls, ten pounds**. We can count them. We cannot say ~~two waters, three musics, one money~~. We cannot count them.

1   Countable nouns can be singular or plural.
This cup is full.
These cups are empty.

Uncountable nouns can only be singular.
The water is cold.
The weather was terrible.

2   Countable nouns are used with **some** + a plural noun in positive sentences, and **any** + a plural noun in questions and negatives.
I've got some books.
Are there any eggs?
We don't need any potatoes.

Uncountable nouns are used with **some** in positive sentences and **any** in questions and negatives, but only with a singular noun.
There is some milk.
Is there any butter?
We haven't got any wine.

3   Countable nouns are used with **many** in questions and negatives.
How many girls were there?
We haven't got many apples.

Uncountable nouns are used with **much** in questions and negatives.
How much money have you got?
There isn't much sugar.

4   Both countable and uncountable nouns are used with **a lot of** and **lots of** in positive sentences.
We've got a lot of eggs.
There are lots of oranges.
There's a lot of milk.
He's got lots of money.

5   Countable nouns are used with **a few**.
I've got a few problems at the moment.

Uncountable nouns are used with **a little**.
We only need a little milk.

Articles

Read this Grammar section as you do the Presentation exercise on page 28. After each rule, there is a letter (A, B, C, etc.). This will help you to identify the different rules.

A and *the*

The indefinite article (**a** or **an**) is used with singular, countable nouns to refer to a thing or an idea for the first time. (A)
We have a cat and a dog.
There's a supermarket in Adam Street.
I'm reading a good book.

The definite article (**the**) is used with singular and plural, countable and uncountable nouns when both the speaker and the listener know the thing or idea already. (B)
We have a cat and a dog. The cat is old, but the dog is just a puppy.
I'm going to the supermarket. Do you want anything? (We both know which supermarket.)
The book is by Mark Anton. (This is the book I was telling you about.)

Indefinite article

The indefinite article is used
1   with professions. (C)
I'm a teacher.
She's an architect.
2   with some expressions of quantity. (D)
a pair of (shoes)   **a little**
a couple of (minutes)   **a few**
a hundred   a thousand
three times a day
forty miles an hour
3   in exclamations with **what** + a countable noun. (E)
What a lovely day!
What a pity!
What a terrible hat!

> **Note**
> In some languages, **one** and **a/an** are the same word. In English, **a/an** for the indefinite is more common. We use **one** if we want to be precise, and we want to emphasize one, not two, or three, or four.
> *He drives a Volkswagen.*
> *She's got one Rolls-Royce, two Cadillacs, and three motorbikes.*

Definite article

The definite article is used
1   before seas, rivers, hotels, pubs, theatres, museums, and newspapers. (F)
the Atlantic   the British Museum
The Times   the Ritz
2   if there is only one. (G)
the sun   the Queen   the Government
3   with superlative adjectives. (H)
He's the richest man in the world.
Jane's the oldest in the class.

> **Note**
> We do not use **the** with parts of the body. We use **my/his/her/your**, etc.
> *I washed my hair.*
> *He broke his leg.*
> **Wrong** He broke ~~the~~ leg.

No article

There is no article
1   before plural and uncountable nouns when talking about things in general. (I)
I like potatoes.
I like bread.
Milk is good for you.
2   before countries, towns, streets, languages, magazines, meals, airports, stations, and mountains. (J)
I had lunch with John.
I bought Cosmopolitan at Paddington Station.
3   before some places and with some forms of transport. (K)
at home   in/to bed   at/to work
at/to school   by bus
by plane   by car   by train   on foot
She goes to work by bus.
I was at home yesterday evening.

> **Note**
> In the phrase **go home**, there is no arcticle and no preposition.
> *I went home early.*
> **Wrong** I went ~~to~~ home.

4   in exclamations with **what** + an uncountable noun. (L)
What beautiful weather!
What loud music!

Can, could, and will

Can, **could**, and **will** are modal auxiliary verbs. They are used with the infinitive (without **to**).
Can I help you?
Could you tell me the time?
I'll carry your bag.

Polite requests

Can and **could** are used for requests.

Can Could	you	pass the salt, please? turn off the TV, please?
Can Could	I	go home, please? have some stamps, please?

Could is (a little) more formal. **Can** is (a little) more familiar.

Offers

Will is used to express an offer of help.
I'll bring some wine.
I'll make you a cup of tea.
John'll take you home.

> **Note**
> 1 In many languages, this use of **will** is sometimes expressed by a present tense. English uses **will** to express an offer made *now* about a future action.
> **Wrong** ~~I give you my phone number.~~
> ~~I open the door for you.~~
> **Right** *I'll give you my phone number.*
> *I'll open the door for you.*
> 2 In this use, the contraction **'ll** is always used.
> **Wrong** ~~I will help you with your homework.~~
> **Right** *I'll help you with your homework.*

Other uses of **will** are in Units 5 and 9. There is more information about modal auxiliary verbs on page 127 of the Grammar section.

> **Note**
> When we ask for things and offer things we use **some** not **any** in the question.
> *Can I have **some** apples, please?*
> *Would you like **some** milk?*
> *Do you want **something** to eat?*

UNIT 5

Verb patterns (1)

Here are three possible verb patterns.
1 Verb + infinitive (+ **to**)
*They **want to buy** a new car.*
*He **promised to come** early.*
*I **decided to go** by taxi.*
*She **forgot to post** the letter.*

2 Verb + **-ing**
*She **enjoys playing** tennis.*
*I **like cooking**, but I **don't like washing up**.*
*Everyone **loves getting** letters.*
*He **finished reading** his book.*

3 Verb + **-ing** or infinitive (+ **to**) with no change in meaning
*It **began to rain/raining**.*
*I **started to learn/learning** English two years ago.*
*I **continued to work/working** in the library.*

Like doing and would like to do

Like doing (and **love doing**) express a general enjoyment.
Would like to do (and **would love to do**) express a preference *now* or at a specific time.
Look at the use of **like** (**love**) and **would like** (**love**) in the following sentences.
*I **like working** as a teacher.* (I am a teacher and I enjoy it.)
*I'd **like to be** a teacher.* (When I grow up, I want to be a teacher.)
*I **love dancing**.* (This is one of my hobbies.)
*Thank you. I'd **love to dance**.* (We're at a disco. I'm pleased that you asked me.)

Short answer
*'**Would** you **like to dance**?'*
*'Yes, I **would**.'/'Yes, I'd **love to**.'*

*'**Would** you **like to come** for a walk?'*
*'Yes, I **would**.'/'No, thank you.'*

> **Note**
> '*No, I **wouldn't**.*' is not common because it is impolite.

There is a list of verb patterns on page 143.

Will

▶ **Form**

will + infinitive (without **to**)
Will is a modal auxiliary verb. There is an introduction to modal auxiliary verbs on page 127 of the Grammar section. The forms of **will** are the same for all persons.

Positive and negative

I She You They etc.	'll (will) won't	come. help you. invite Tom.

Question

When will	he you they etc.	help me?

Short answer
*'**Will** you help me?'*
*'Yes, I **will**.'*

> **Note**
> '*No, I **won't**.*' is not common because it is impolite. It means '*I don't want to help you.*'
> A polite way of saying 'no' here would be '*I'm afraid I can't.*'

▶ **Use**

Will is used
1 to express a future decision or intention made at the moment of speaking.
'It's Jane's birthday.'
'Is it? I'll buy her some flowers.'

Goodbye. I'll see you tomorrow.

'Which do you want? The blue or the red?'
'I'll take the red. Thank you.'

2 to express an offer. This is a similar use to 1.
I'll carry your suitcase.
We'll do the washing-up.
This use is in Unit 4.
Other uses of **will** are in Unit 9.

Going to

▶ **Form**

am is are	+ **going** + **to** + infinitive

Positive and negative

I	'm (am) 'm not	
He She It	's (is) isn't	going to work.
We You They	're (are) aren't	

Question

When	am I		going to arrive?
	is	he she it	
	are	we you they	

Short answer

'*Are they going to get married?*'
'*Yes, they are.*'/'*No, they aren't.*'

▶ **Use**

Going to is used

1 to express a future decision, intention, or plan made before the moment of speaking.
We're going to move to London.
How long are they going to stay in Rome?
She isn't going to have a birthday party.

> **Note**
> The Present Continuous can be used in a similar way for a plan or arrangement, particularly with the verbs **go** and **come**.
> *She's coming on Friday.*
> *I'm going home early tonight.*
> *We're meeting Alan at the airport.*

2 when we can see or feel now that something is certain to happen in the future.
Look at those clouds! It's going to rain.
Watch out! That box is going to fall.
You work so hard. You're going to be rich and successful.

Will or *going to*?

Look at the use of **will** and **going to** in the following sentences.
I'm going to make a chicken casserole for dinner.
(I decided this morning and bought everything for it.)
What shall I cook for dinner? Er . . . I know! I'll make chicken casserole! That's a good idea! (I decided at the moment of speaking.)

UNIT 6

What . . . like?

▶ **Form**

what + verb **to be** + subject + **like?**

What	's (is) your teacher are his parents was your holiday were the beaches	like?

| She's very patient. |
| They're very kind. |
| Wonderful. We swam a lot. |
| OK, but some were dirty. |

> **Note**
> We don't use **like** in the answer.
> **Wrong** She's ~~like~~ patient.
> **Right** *She's patient.*

▶ **Use**

What . . . like? means '*Describe somebody or something. Tell me about them.*'
Like in this question is a preposition, not a verb:
'*What's Jim like?*'
'*He's intelligent and kind, and he's got lovely blue eyes.*'
In the following sentences **like** is a verb:
'*What does Jim like?*'
'*He likes motorbikes and playing tennis.*'

> **Note**
> '*How's your mother?*'
> '*She's very well, thank you.*'
> **How's your mother?** asks about health. It doesn't ask for a description.

Comparative and superlative adjectives

▶ **Form**

		Comparative	Superlative
Short adjectives	cheap small *big	cheaper smaller bigger	cheapest smallest biggest
Adjectives that end in y	funny early heavy	funnier earlier heavier	funniest earliest heaviest
Adjectives with two syllables or more	careful boring expensive interesting	more careful more boring more expensive more interesting	most careful most boring most expensive most interesting
Irregular adjectives	good bad far	better worse further/farther	best worst furthest/farthest

*Short adjectives with one vowel and one consonant double the consonant: *hot/hotter/hottest, fat/fatter/fattest.*

▶ **Use**

1 **Than** is often used after a comparative adjective.
I'm younger than Barbara.
Barbara's more intelligent than Sarah.
Much can come before the comparative to give emphasis.
She's much nicer than her sister.
Is Tokyo much more modern than London?

2 **The** is used before superlative adjectives.
He's the funniest boy in the class.
Which is the tallest building in the world?

3 **As . . . as** shows that something is the same or equal.
Jim's as tall as Peter.
I'm as worried as you are.

4 **Not as/so . . . as** shows that something isn't the same or equal.
She isn't as tall as her mother.
My car wasn't so expensive as yours.

UNIT 7

Present Perfect Simple

▶ Form

have/has + verb + **-ed** (past participle)
The past participle of regular verbs ends in **-ed**. There are many common irregular verbs. See the list on page 141.

Positive and negative

I We You They	've (have) haven't	worked in a factory.
He She It	's (has) hasn't	

Question

Have	I we you they	been to the United States?
Has	he she it	

Short answer
'*Have you been* to Egypt?'
'Yes, I *have*.'/'No, I *haven't*.'

'*Has she ever written* poetry?'
'Yes, she *has*.'/'No, she *hasn't*.'

> **Note**
> We cannot use **I've, they've, he's**, etc. in short answers.
> **Wrong** Yes, I've.
> Yes, we've.
> **Right** Yes, I *have*.
> Yes, we *have*.

▶ Use

The Present Perfect relates past actions and states to the present.
The Present Perfect is in a sense a present tense. It looks back from the present into the past, and expresses what has happened *before now*.
I've met a lot of famous people. (before now)
She's lived here all her life. (up to the present, and probably into the future)

Here are two main uses of the Present Perfect:
1 to express an action in the past. We are interested in the experience as part of someone's life.
I've travelled a lot in Africa.
They've lived all over the world.

Ever and **never** are common with this use.
Have you ever been in a car crash?
My mother has never flown in a plane.

2 to express an action or state which began in the past and continues to the present.
I've known Alice for six years.
How long have you worked as a teacher?

For and **since** are common with this use.
We've lived here for two years.
I've had a beard since I left the army.

> **Note**
> In many languages, this use is expressed by a present tense. In a way, this is logical. 'Peter is a teacher. Peter is a teacher for ten years.' But English has a tense which looks back from the present to the past, the Present Perfect. So we say '*Peter has been*...'.
> **Wrong** Peter is a teacher for ten years.
> **Right** Peter *has been* a teacher for ten years.

Present Perfect and Past Simple

1 Look at the use of the Present Perfect and the Past Simple in the following sentences.
I've lived in Rome for six months. (I still do.)
I lived in London for a year. (Now I live somewhere else, not in London.)
Sally's written several books. (She's still alive.)
Shakespeare wrote many plays. (He is dead.)
He's worked in the bank for three years.
He started working in the bank in 1989/when he was 20/three years ago.

2 Look at the wrong sentences and compare them with the right sentences.

×	I've broken my leg last year.
√	I broke my leg last year.
×	He works as a musician all his life.
√	He has worked as a musician all his life.
×	When have you been to Greece?
√	When did you go to Greece?
×	How long do you have your car?
√	How long have you had your car?

There is more information about the Present Perfect on page 131 of the Grammar section.

UNIT 8

Have to

▶ Form

has
have | + **to** + infinitive
The form is the same as **have** + **do/does/did** to express possession (see page 121).

Positive and negative

I We You They	have don't have	to work hard.
He She It	has doesn't have	

Question

Do	I we you they	have to work hard?
Does	he she it	

Short answer
'*Do you have to wear* a uniform?'
'Yes, I *do*.'

'*Does he have to go* now?'
'No, he *doesn't*.'

> **Note**
> The past tense of **have to** is **had to**, with **did** and **didn't** in the question and the negative.
> *I had to get up* early this morning.
> *Why did you have to work* last weekend?
> *They liked the hotel because they didn't have to do* any cooking.

▶ Use

Have to expresses strong obligation. The obligation comes from 'outside' – perhaps a law, a rule at school or work, or someone in authority.
You have to have a driving licence if you want to drive a car.
I have to start work at 8.00.
The doctor says I have to do more exercise.

Don't/doesn't have to expresses absence of obligation (it *isn't* necessary).
You don't have to do the washing-up. I've got a dishwasher.
She doesn't have to work on Mondays.

Note

1 **Must** is also used to express strong obligation. Generally, when it is used, the obligation comes from the speaker.
   *I **must** get my hair cut.*
   This suggests that *I* feel it is necessary.

2 **You must** ... can be used to express a strong suggestion.
   *You **must see** the Monet exhibition! It's wonderful!*
   *You **must give** me a ring when you're next in town.*

Introduction to modal auxiliary verbs

▶ **Form**

The following are modal auxiliary verbs.

can   could   might   must
shall should   will   would

They are dealt with in different units of *Headway*.
They have the following in common:

1 They 'help' another verb. The verb form is the infinitive (without **to**).
   *She **can** drive.*
   *I **must** get my hair cut.*
   *You **should tell** the truth.*
   Wrong I can ~~to~~ swim.
              I must ~~to~~ go.
   Right *I **can** swim.*
              *I **must** go.*

2 There is no **do/does** in the question.
   Can she type?
   ***Should** I go home now?*
   Wrong ~~Do~~ you ~~can~~ type?
   Right *Can you type?*

3 The form is the same for all persons. There is no **-s** in the third person singular.
   *He **can** dance very well.*
   *She **should** try harder.*
   *It **will** rain soon.*
   Wrong He can~~s~~ dance.
   Right *He **can** dance.*

4 To form the negative, add **n't**. There is no **don't/doesn't**.
   *I **can't** spell.*
   *I **wouldn't** like to be a teacher.*
   *You **mustn't** steal.*
   Wrong I do~~n't~~ can help you.
   Right *I **can't** help you.*

Note
will not = **won't**.
*It **won't** rain tomorrow.*

5 Most modal verbs refer to the present and future. Only **can** has a past tense form, **could**.
   *I **could** swim when I was three.*

Should

▶ **Form**

should + infinitive (without **to**)
The forms of **should** are the same for all persons.

Positive and negative

I He We They etc.	should do more exercise. shouldn't tell lies.

Question

Should	I she they		see a doctor?
Do you think	I he we	should	

Short answer
'***Should** I phone home?*'
'*Yes, you **should**.*'

'***Should** I buy a Mercedes Benz?*'
'*No, you **shouldn't**.*'

▶ **Use**

Should is used to express what the speaker thinks is right or the best thing to do. It expresses mild obligation, or advice.
*I **should** do more work.* (This is my opinion.)
*You **should** do more work.* (I'm telling you what I think.)
*Do you think we **should** stop here?* (I'm asking you for your opinion.)

Shouldn't expresses negative advice.
*You **shouldn't** sit so close to the TV. It's bad for your eyes.*

Note
Should expresses the opinion of the speaker, and it is often introduced by **I think** or **I don't think**.
*I **think** politicians **should** listen more.*
*I **don't think** people **should** get married until they're 21.*

UNIT 9

Will

▶ **Form**

will + infinitive (without **to**)
Will is a modal auxiliary verb. For an introduction to modal auxiliary verbs, see the first column on this page.

Positive and negative

I She You They etc.	'll (will) won't	arrive next week.

Question

When will	he you etc.	arrive?

Short answer
'***Will** you **be** here next week?*'
'*Yes, I **will**.*'

'***Will** the meal **be** expensive?*'
'*No, it **won't**.*'

▶ **Use**

Will is used

1 to express a future intention or decision made at the moment of speaking.
   I'll have a steak, please.
   I'll give you your book back tomorrow.

2 to express a future fact. The speaker thinks '*This action is sure to happen sometime in the future*'.
   *Liverpool **will** win the cup.*
   *The Queen **will** open the new hospital next Thursday.*

First Conditional

▶ **Form**

if + Present Simple, **will** + infinitive (without **to**)

Positive and negative

If	I work hard, I she has enough money, she we don't hurry up, we	'll (will)	pass my exams. buy a new car. be late.
If	you're late, I	won't	wait for you.

Question

| What | will | you do | if | you don't go to university? |
| Where | | she go | | she can't find a job? |

Short answer

'*Will you go to university if you pass your exams?*'
'*Yes, I will.*'/'*No, I won't.*'

'*If we look after the planet, will we survive?*'
'*Yes, we will.*'/'*No, we won't.*'

> **Note**
> The condition clause (**if** . . .) can come at the beginning of the sentence or at the end.
> *I'll pass my exams if I work hard.*
> *If I work hard, I'll pass my exams.*

▶ **Use**

The First Conditional is used to express a possible condition and a probable result in the future.
If my cheque comes, I'll buy us all a meal.
You'll get wet if you don't take an umbrella.
What'll happen to the environment if we don't look after it?

> **Note**
> English uses a present tense in the condition clause, not a future form.
> **Wrong** If it will rain . . .
>   If I'll work hard . . .
> **Right** If it *rains* . . .
>   If I *work* hard . . .

Time clauses

▶ **Form**

Conjunction + Present Simple, **will** + infinitive (without **to**)
Conjunctions of time (e.g. **when**, **as soon as**, **before**, **until**) are not usually followed by **will**. The clause refers to the future, but English uses the Present Simple, not **will**.
When our guests arrive, we'll eat.
As soon as I have some news, I'll phone you.
I'll do my work after I have (or have had) a bath.
I'll speak to you again before I leave.
We'll stay here until the rain stops.

> **Note**
> **If** expresses a possibility that something will happen; **when** expresses what the speaker sees as certain to happen.
> *If I find your book, I'll send it to you.*
> *When I get home, I'll have a bath.*

UNIT 10

Used to

▶ **Form**

used + **to** + infinitive
Used to is the same in all persons.

Positive and negative

| I She They etc. | used to didn't use to | smoke. like cooking. |

Question

| What did you use to do? |

Short answer

'*Did you use to smoke a lot?*'
'*Yes, I did.*'/'*No, I didn't.*'

> **Note**
> 1 The question form is not often used. We ask a question in the Past Simple, and reply using **used to**.
>   '*Where did you go on holiday when you were young?*'
>   '*We used to go camping in France.*'
> 2 **Never** is often used.
>   *I never used to watch TV.*
> 3 **Be careful** not to confuse **to use** (e.g. *I use a knife to cut an apple.*) and **used to**.
>   The pronunciation is also different.
>   to use /juːz/
>   used to /juːstʊ/ or /juːstə/

▶ **Use**

Used to is used
1 to express a past habit.
   He used to play football every Saturday, but now he doesn't.
2 to express a past state.
   They used to be happy together, but now they fight all the time.

Used to and the Past Simple

The Past Simple can also be used for a past habit or state.
He played football every Sunday when he was a boy.
They were happy together when they were first married.

Only the Past Simple can be used for actions which happened once in the past.

We used to go to France every summer, but once, in 1987, we went to Greece.

Last night I drank champagne.

> **Note**
> **Used to** has no equivalent in the present. The Present Simple is used for present habits and states.
> *She lives in New York.*
> *She sometimes comes to London on business.*

Subject questions

▶ **Form**

The question words **who** and **what** can be used as both the subject and the object in a sentence.

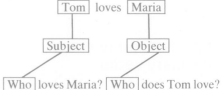

In subject questions, there is no inversion, and no **do/does/did**. Look at the following examples of subject and object questions.

Subject
1 Who broke the window?
2 Who has been to the States?
3 Who told you the news?
4 What's making that noise?
5 What happened to your eye?

Object
1 What did you break?
2 Who did you meet in the States?
3 Who did you talk to?
4 Who are you inviting to the party?
5 What did you do to your eye?

UNIT 11

The passive

▶ Form

| am/is/are
was/were
has/have been | + verb + **-ed** (past
participle) |

The past participle of regular verbs ends in
-ed. There are many common irregular
verbs. See the list on page 141.

Present

Positive and negative
*English **is spoken** all over the world.*
*Renault cars **are made** in France.*
*My children **aren't helped** with their*
  homework.
*Coffee **isn't grown** in England.*

Question
*Where **is** rice **grown**?*
*Are cars **made** in your country?*

Past

Positive and negative
*My car **was stolen** last night.*
*The animals **were frightened** by a loud*
  noise.
*He **wasn't injured** in the accident.*
*The thieves **weren't seen** by anyone.*

Question
*How **was** the window **broken**?*
*Were the plants **watered** last night?*

Present Perfect

Positive and negative
*I've **been robbed**!*
*Diet Coke **has been made** since 1982.*

Question
*How many times **have** you **been hurt***
  playing football?
*Has my car **been repaired**?*

Short answer
*'Are cars **made** in your country?'*
*'Yes, they **are**.'/'No, they **aren't**.'*

*'Were the plants **watered** last night?'*
*'Yes, they **were**.'/'No, they **weren't**.'*

*'Has my car **been repaired**?'*
*'Yes, it **has**.'/'No, it **hasn't**.'*

Note
1 The rules for tense usage in the
   passive are the same as in the
   active.
   Present Simple to express habit:
   *My car **is serviced** regularly.*
   Past Simple to express a finished
   action in the past:
   *America **was discovered** by*
   Christopher Columbus.
   Present Perfect to express an
   action which began in the past and
   continues to the present:
   *Diet Coke **has been made** since*
   1982.
2 The passive infinitive (**to be** + verb
   + **-ed**) is used after modal auxiliary
   verbs and other verbs which are
   followed by an infinitive.
   *Driving **should be banned** in city*
   centres.
   *The house **is going to be knocked***
   down.

▶ Use

1 The object of an active verb becomes
   the subject of a passive verb.

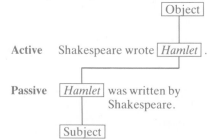

2 The passive is not another way of
   expressing the same sentence in the
   active. We choose the active or the
   passive depending on what we are more
   interested in.
   *Hamlet **was written** in 1600.* (We are
   more interested in *Hamlet*.)
   *Shakespeare **wrote** comedies, histories,*
   and tragedies. (We are more interested
   in Shakespeare.)

Note
Some verbs, for example, **give**, have
two objects, a person and a thing.
*She gave **me** a **book** for my birthday.*
In the passive, we often make the
person the subject, not the thing.
*I **was given** a **book** for my birthday.*

UNIT 12

Verb patterns (2)

We saw several verb patterns in Unit 5.
Here are some more examples.
1 Verb + infinitive (+ **to**)
   *She **agreed to help** me.*
   *We **chose to go** by coach because it was*
   cheaper.
   *I **expect to hear** from you soon.*
   *He **refused to believe** me.*
2 Verb + person + infinitive (+ **to**)
   *I **advise you to do** nothing.*
   *She **helped me to tidy** up.*
   *My parents **encouraged me to go** to*
   university.
   *They **invited me to spend** the weekend*
   with them.
   *I **want you to learn** this for homework.*
3 Verb + person + infinitive (without **to**)
   *My teachers **made me work** hard.*
   *My parents **let me stay** up as long as I*
   want.

Note
Start and **begin** can be followed by the
infinitive or **-ing** with no change in
meaning. If the first verb is in the
continuous, English prefers the
infinitive.
Wrong ~~It's starting raining.~~
Right *It's **starting to rain**.*

There is a list of verb patterns on page 143.

Infinitives

1 Infinitives are used after certain
   adjectives.

| I'm | pleased
surprised | to see you. |

| It's | hard
important
impossible | to learn Chinese. |

2 Infinitives are used to express purpose.
   They answer the question **Why?** This
   use is very common in English.
   *I'm learning English **to get** a good job.*
   *She's saving her money **to buy** a car.*
   *I'm going to Scotland **to visit** my parents.*

Note
Some languages express this idea of
purpose with a translation of **for** +
infinitive. English does not use **for**.
Wrong ~~I came here for to learn~~
        ~~English.~~
Right *I came here **to learn** English.*

UNIT 13

Second Conditional

▶ Form

if + Past Simple, **would** + infinitive (without **to**)
Would is a modal auxiliary verb. There is an introduction to modal auxiliary verbs on page 127 of the Grammar section.
The forms of **would** are the same for all persons.

Positive and negative

If	I had more money, I she knew the answer, she we lived in Russia, we

	'd (would)	buy a CD player. tell us. soon learn Russian.

If I didn't have so many debts, I wouldn't have to work so hard.

Question

What Which countries	would	you do you go to

	if	you had a year off? you travelled round the world?

Short answer
'*Would* you *travel* round the world?'
'*Yes, I would.*'/'*No, I wouldn't.*'

'*If* they *had* the money, *would* they *buy* a new car?'
'*Yes, they would.*'/'*No, they wouldn't.*'

> **Note**
> 1 The condition clause can come at the beginning of the sentence or at the end.
> *I'd help if I had more time.*
> *If I had more time, I'd help.*
> 2 **Were** is often used instead of **was** in the condition clause.
> *If I were you, I'd go to bed.*
> *If he were cleverer, he'd know he was making a mistake.*

▶ Use

The Second Conditional is used to express an unreal or improbable condition and its probable result in the present or future. The condition is unreal because it is different from the facts that we know. We can always say '*But . . .*'

If I were Prime Minister, I'd increase tax for rich people. (But I'm not Prime Minister.)
If I lived in a big house, I'd have a party. (But I live in a small house.)
What would you do if you saw a ghost? (But I don't expect that you will see a ghost.)

> **Note**
> 1 The use of the Past Tense (**If I had**) and **would** does not refer to past time. Both the First Conditional and the Second Conditional refer to the present and the future. The past verb forms are used to show '*This is different from reality*'.
>
> *If I win the tennis match, I'll be happy.* (I think I have a good chance.)
> *If I won a thousand pounds, I'd . . .* (But I don't think I will.)
> 2 We do not use **would** in the condition clause.
> **Wrong** If I ~~would have~~ more money . . .
> If the weather ~~would be~~ nice . . .
> **Right** *If I had more money, . . .*
> *If the weather was nice, . . .*

Might

▶ Form

might + infinitive (without **to**)
Might is a modal auxiliary verb. For an introduction to modal auxiliary verbs, see page 127 in the Grammar section.
The forms of **might** are the same for all persons.

Positive and negative

I He It We etc.	might might not	go to the party. be late. rain tomorrow. go out for a meal tonight.

The contraction **mightn't** is unusual.

Question
The inverted question **Might you . . .?** is unusual. It is very common to ask a question with **Do you think . . . + will . . . ?**

Do you think	you'll get here on time? it'll rain? they'll come to our party?

Short answer
'*Do you think he'll come?*'
'*He might.*'

'*Do you think it'll rain?*'
'*It might.*'

▶ Use

Might is used to express a future possibility. It contrasts with **will**, which, in the speaker's opinion, expresses a future certainty.
England will win the match. (I am sure they will.)
England might win the match. (It's possible, but I don't know.)

> **Note**
> Notice that, in the negative, the following sentences express the same idea of possibility.
> *It might not rain this afternoon.*
> *I don't think it'll rain this afternoon.*

UNIT 14

Present Perfect Simple (2)

▶ Form

For the form of the Present Perfect Simple, see page 126 of the Grammar section.

▶ Use

Re-read the Grammar section on the Present Perfect Simple on page 126. The Present Perfect Simple looks back from the present to the past.
In this unit, we see that the Present Perfect is used to express a past action with a result in the present. We are looking at a recent past action, and expressing its effect on the present.

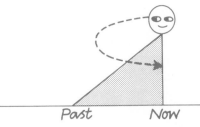

I've lost my wallet. (I haven't got it now.)
My car's been stolen! (It isn't here now.)
Has the postman brought any letters? (Are there any letters on the mat now?)

> **Note**
> Notice the use of certain adverbs with this use of the Present Perfect.
> *She's just passed her driving test.* (a very short time before)
> *Thanks, but I've already had lunch.* (some time before now)
> *Has the postman been yet?* (any time before now)
> *He hasn't got up yet*, and it's 11.00! (**Yet** is used in questions and negative sentences.)

Present Perfect Continuous

▶ Form

has
have } + **been** + verb + **-ing** (present participle)

Positive and negative

I We You They	've (have) haven't	
He She It	's (has) hasn't	been working.

Question

How long	have	I we you they	been working?
	has	he she it	

Short answer

'*Have you been running?*'
'*Yes, I have.*'/'*No, I haven't.*'

'*Has he been shopping?*'
'*Yes, he has.*'/'*No, he hasn't.*'

▶ Use

The Present Perfect Continuous is used
1 to express an activity which continues to the present.
We've been waiting here for hours!
It's been raining for days.
2 to refer to an activity with a result in the present.
I'm hot because I've been running.
Her shoes are muddy. She's been digging the garden.

> **Note**
> 1 Sometimes there is little or no difference in meaning between the Present Perfect Simple and Continuous.
> *How long* **have** *you* **worked** *here?*
> *How long* **have** *you* **been working** *here?*
> 2 Think of the verbs that have the idea of a long time, for example, *wait, work, learn, travel, play*. These verbs can be found in the Present Perfect Continuous.
> *I've been playing tennis since I was a boy.*
> Think of the verbs that *don't* have the idea of a long time, for example, *find, start, buy, die, lose, break, stop*. It is unusual to find these verbs in the Present Perfect Continuous.
> *I've bought a new dress.*
> *My cat has died.*
> *My radio's broken.*
> 3 Verbs that express a state (for example, *like, love, know, have* for possession) are not found in the Present Perfect Continuous.
> *We've known each other for a few weeks.*
> *How long have you had your car?*
> **Wrong** We've been knowing each other for a few weeks.
> 4 The Present Perfect Simple looks at the completed action. This is why, if the sentence gives a number or a quantity, the Present Perfect Simple is used.
> *I've written three letters today.*
> The Continuous is not possible.
> **Wrong** I've been writing three letters today.

UNIT 15

Past Perfect

▶ Form

had + verb + **-ed** (past participle)

The past participle of regular verbs ends in **-ed**. There are many common irregular verbs. See the list on page 141.

Positive and negative

I He She It We You They	'd (had) hadn't	arrived before 10.00.

Question

Had	I he she it we you they	left?

Short answer

'*Had the play already started when you arrived?*'
'*Yes, it had.*'/'*No, it hadn't.*'

▶ Use

The Past Perfect is used to express an action in the past which happened *before* another action in the past.

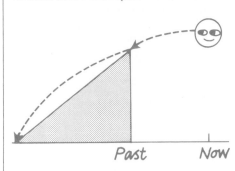

When I got home, John had already cleaned the house and cooked a meal.

> **Note**
> Notice the use of the Past Perfect and the Past Simple in the following sentences.
> *When I got home, John cooked a meal.* (First I got home, then John cooked.)
> *When I got home, John had cooked a meal.* (John cooked a meal *before* I got home.)

Reported statements

▶ **Form**

The usual rule is that the verb form moves 'one tense back'.

Present → past
'*I love you.*' → *He said he loved me.*
'*I'm going out now.*' → *Ann said she was going out.*

Present Perfect → Past Perfect
'*We've met before.*' → *She said they'd met before.*

Past Simple → Past Perfect
'*We met in 1987.*' → *He said they'd met in 1987.*

Will → would
'*I'll mend it for you.*' → *She said that she would mend it for me.*

Can → could
'*I can swim.*' → *She said she could swim.*

Reported questions

▶ **Form**

The verb form also moves 'one tense back'.

Present → past
'*Do you like school?*' → *He asked me if I liked school.*

Present Perfect → Past Perfect
'*Have you met my wife?*' → *He asked if I had met his wife.*

> **Note**
> The word order in the reported question is the same as the statement. There is no **do/does/did**.
>
> I was going home.
> He asked me where I was going .
>
> She lived in Rome.
> I asked her where she lived .

Word list

Here is a list of words that appear unit by unit in *Headway Pre-Intermediate*. You can write in the translation if you want. Most of the new words are here, but if a word isn't very useful or very common, it isn't in these lists. Words are repeated if they come in a later unit, and if we think it's a good idea to revise them.

Abbreviations

adj = adjective	*prep* = preposition
n = noun	*pp* = past participle
v = verb	*opp* = opposite
adv = adverb	*det* = determiner (e.g. *some*, *several*)

UNIT 1

bilingual (*adj*)   /baɪ'lɪŋgwəl/
book(*v*) (a seat)   /bʊk/
boot(*n*)   /buːt/
born (*pp*)   /bɔːn/
branch (*n*) (of a tree)   /brɑːntʃ/
branch (*n*) (of a shop)   /brɑːntʃ/

calculator (*n*)   /'kælkjʊleɪtə(r)/
castle (*n*)   /'kɑːsl/
change (*n*) (money)   /tʃeɪndʒ/
chewing gum (*n*)   /'tʃuːɪŋ gʌm/
choose (*v*)   /tʃuːz/
coast (*n*)   /kəʊst/
comb (*n*)   /kəʊm/
course (*n*) (of study)   /kɔːs/

earth (*n*)   /ɜːθ/
elect (*v*)   /ɪ'lekt/
enjoy (*v*)   /ɪn'dʒɔɪ/
equator (*n*)   /ɪ'kweɪtə(r)/

fan (*n*) (for air)   /fæn/
fan (*n*) (a person)   /fæn/
file (*n*) (for papers)   /faɪl/
flat (*n*) (to live)   /flæt/
flat (*adj*) (surface)   /flæt/

get married (*v*)   /get 'mærɪd/
glasses (*n*)   /'glɑːsɪz/

hanky (*n*)   /'hæŋkɪ/
hear (*v*)   /hɪə(r)/

ice (*n*)   /aɪs/

joke (*n*)   /dʒəʊk/
jungle (*n*)   /'dʒʌŋgl/

kind (*n*) (= sort)   /kaɪnd/
kind (*adj*) (= nice)   /kaɪnd/

laugh (*v*)   /lɑːf/
leave (*v*)   /liːv/
lighter (*n*)   /'laɪtə/
lipstick (*n*)   /'lɪpstɪk/
look after (*v*)   /lʊk'ɑːftə(r)/

mean (*v*) (What does it mean?)   /miːn/
mean (*adj*) (opp = generous)   /miːn/

part-time (*adj*)   /pɑ:t'taɪm/
plaster (*n*)   /'plɑ:stə(r)/
play (*v*) (a game)   /pleɪ/
play (*n*) (in the theatre)   /pleɪ/
poetry (*n*)   /'pəʊɪtrɪ/
powerful (*adj*)   /'paʊəfl/
purse (*n*)   /pɜ:s/

receipt (*n*)   /rɪ'si:t/
record (*v*)   /rɪ'kɔ:d/
ring (*v*) (= phone)   /rɪŋ/
ring (*n*) (on your finger)   /rɪŋ/

safe (*adj*)   /seɪf/
scissors (*n*)   /'sɪzəz/
season ticket (*n*)   /'si:zn tɪkɪt/
single (*adj*)   /sɪŋgl/
sink (*v*) (in water)   /sɪŋk/
sink (*n*) (in kitchen)   /sɪŋk/
smell (*v*)   /smel/
strike (*v*) (= hit)   /straɪk/
strike (*n*) (not work)   /straɪk/
surname (*n*)   /'sɜ:neɪm/

tap (*v*) (touch)   /tæp/
tap (*n*) (on a sink)   /tæp/
T-shirt (*n*)   /'ti:ʃɜ:t/

wallet (*n*)   /'wɒlɪt/
worried (*adj*)   /'wʌrɪd/

UNIT 2

adapt (*v*)   /ə'dæpt/
addicted (*adj*)   /ə'dɪktɪd/
air conditioning (*n*)   /'eə kəndɪʃnɪŋ/
attitude (*n*)   /'ætɪtju:d/

babysit (*v*)   /'beɪbɪsɪt/
bored (*adj*)   /bɔ:d/
borrow (*v*)   /'bɒrəʊ/
bride (*n*)   /braɪd/

CD player (*n*)   /si: 'di: pleɪjə(r)/
company (*n*) (= business)   /'kʌmpənɪ/
complaint (*n*)   /kəm'pleɪnt/
computer (*n*)   /kəm'pju:tə(r)/
cooker (*n*)   /'kʊkə(r)/
crèche (*n*)   /kreʃ/
credit card (*n*)   /'kredɪt kɑ:d/

discover (*n*)   /dɪs'kʌvə(r)/
dishwasher (*n*)   /'dɪʃwɒʃə(r)/
divorced (*pp*)   /dɪ'vɔ:st/
dozen (*n*)   /dʌzn/

employment (*n*)   /ɪm'plɔɪmənt/
exchange rate (*n*)   /ɪks'tʃeɪndʒ reɪt/

flag (*n*)   /flæg/
fluently (*adj*)   /'flu:əntlɪ/
fog (*n*)   /fɒg/
food mixer (*n*)   /'fu:d mɪksə(r)/
freedom (*n*)   /'fri:dəm/
freezer (*n*)   /'fri:zə(r)/
fridge (*n*)   /frɪdʒ/
full-time (*adj*)   /fʊl'taɪm/

health (*n*)   /helθ/
hi-fi (*n*)   /'haɪfaɪ/

interview (*v* and *n*)   /'ɪntəvju:/
iron (*n*)   /'aɪən/

kettle (*n*)   /'ketl/

lamp (*n*)   /læmp/
lifestyle (*n*)   /'laɪfstaɪl/
litter (*n*)   /'lɪtə(r)/

microwave oven (*n*)   /'maɪkrəweɪv 'ʌvn/
miserable (*adj*)   /'mɪzrəbl/

rarely (*adj*)   /'reəlɪ/
relax (*v*)   /rɪ'læks/
research (*n*)   /rɪ'sɜ:tʃ/
retired (*adj*)   /rɪ'taɪəd/
rude (*adj*)   /ru:d/

save (*v*)   /seɪv/
shower (*n*)   /ʃaʊə(r)/
spotlight (*n*)   /'spɒtlaɪt/
standard of living (*n*)   /'stændəd əv 'lɪvɪŋ/
stereo (*n*)   /'sterɪəʊ/
strict (*adj*)   /strɪkt/

unemployment (*n*)   /ʌnɪm'plɔɪmənt/
unusual (*adj*)   /ʌn'ju:ʒl/

vacuum cleaner (*n*)   /'vækjʊəm kli:nə(r)/
video (*n*)   /'vɪdɪəʊ/

Walkman (*n*)   /'wɔ:kmən/
washing machine (*n*)   /'wɒʃɪŋ məʃi:n/
word processor (*n*)   /'wɜ:d prəʊsesə(r)/
worry (*v*)   /'wʌrɪ/

UNIT 3

agree (*v*) (with sb)   /ə'gri:/
army (*n*)   /'ɑ:mɪ/
author (*n*)   /'ɔ:θə(r)/

bill (*n*) (in a restaurant)   /bɪl/
biography (*n*)   /baɪ'ɒgrəfɪ/
breathe (*v*)   /bri:ð/

catch (*v*) (fish)   /kætʃ/
champion (*n*)   /'tʃæmpɪən/
creep (*v*)   /kri:p/
describe (*v*)   /dɪs'kraɪb/
description (*n*)   /dɪ'skrɪpʃn/
do the washing-up (*v*)   /du: ðə wɒʃɪŋ 'ʌp/
draw (*v*) (a picture)   /drɔ:/

escape (*v* and *n*)   /ɪ'skeɪp/

fall (*v*)   /fɔ:l/
feel (*v*)   /fi:l/
fish (*v* and *n*)   /fɪʃ/

gun (*n*)   /gʌn/

healthy (*adj*)   /'helθɪ/
hero (*n*)   /'hɪərəʊ/

lie (n) (opp = truth)   /laɪ/
look at (v)   /'lʊk ət/
look for (v)   /'lʊk fə(r)/

midnight (n)   /'mɪdnaɪt/

novel (n)   /'nɒvl/

pack (v) (a suitcase)   /pæk/
pass (v) (an exam)   /pɑ:s/
peaceful (adj)   /'pi:sfl/
pillow (n)   /'pɪləʊ/
point (v)   /pɔɪnt/

raw (adj)   /rɔ:/
rock (n)   /rɒk/

shark (n)   /ʃɑ:k/
similar (adj)   /'sɪmɪlə(r)/
sink (v)   /sɪŋk/
soldier (n)   /'səʊldʒə(r)/
spend (v) (time)   /spend/
spy (n)   /spaɪ/
stockbroker (n)   /'stɒkbrəʊkə(r)/
suit (n)   /su:t/
survive (v)   /sə'vaɪv/

throw (v)   /θrəʊ/
tin (n) (of food)   /tɪn/

van (n)   /væn/

waterfall (n)   /'wɔ:təfɔ:l/
whale (n)   /weɪl/
whisper (n)   /'wɪspə(r)/

yacht (n)   /jɒt/

UNIT 4

advertisement (n)   /əd'vɜ:tɪsmənt/
advise (v)   /əd'vaɪz/

bake (v)   /beɪk/
boil (v)   /bɔɪl/
bowl (n)   /bəʊl/
bra (n)   /brɑ:/
Brussels sprout (n)   /brʌsl 'spraʊt/

cabbage (n)   /'kæbɪdʒ/
carrot (n)   /'kærət/
cauliflower (n)   /'kɒliflaʊə(r)/
celery (n)   /'seləri/
charge (v) (money)   /tʃɑ:dʒ/
cherry (n)   /'tʃeri/
chicken (n)   /'tʃɪkɪn/
chop (v) (with a knife)   /tʃɒp/
chop (n) (cut of meat)   /tʃɒp/
cucumber (n)   /'kju:kʌmbə(r)/

department store (n)   /dɪ'pɑ:tmənt stɔ:(r)/
designer (n)   /dɪ'zaɪnə(r)/
dessert (n)   /dɪ'zɜ:t/
dinner party (n)   /'dɪnə pɑ:ti/
dish (n)   /dɪʃ/
dressing gown (n)   /'dresɪŋ gaʊn/

flour (n)   /flaʊə(r)/
fry (v)   /fraɪ/
frying-pan (n)   /'fraɪɪŋ pæn/

garlic (n)   /'gɑ:lɪk/
grape (n)   /greɪp/
greasy (adj) (hair)   /'gri:si/
grill (v)   /grɪl/

immigrant (n)   /'ɪmɪgrənt/
ingredient (n)   /ɪn'gri:dɪənt/

jumper (n) (to wear)   /'dʒʌmpə(r)/

knickers (n)   /'nɪkəz/

label (n) (on a suitcase)   /'leɪbl/
lettuce (n)   /'letɪs/

melon (n)   /'melən/
minced beef (n)   /mɪnst 'bi:f/
mushroom (n)   /'mʌʃru:m/

onion (n)   /'ʌnɪən/
oven (n)   /ʌvn/

peach (n)   /pi:tʃ/
peel (v)   /pi:l/
pie (n)   /paɪ/
pineapple (n)   /'paɪnæpl/
potato (n)   /pə'teɪtəʊ/
profit (n)   /'prɒfɪt/

raisin (n)   /'reɪzn/
raspberry (n)   /'rɑ:zbri/
recipe (n)   /'resəpi/
roast (v)   /rəʊst/

saucepan (n)   /'sɔ:spən/
shampoo (n)   /ʃæm'pu:/
shopkeeper (n)   /'ʃɒpki:pə(r)/
slice (v and n)   /slaɪs/
soft drink (n)   /sɒf 'drɪŋk/
squeeze (v)   /skwi:z/
stall (n) (in a market)   /stɔ:l/
strawberry (n)   /'strɔ:bri/
sultana (n)   /sʌl'tɑ:nə/

train (v) (for a job)   /treɪn/

underwear (n)   /'ʌndəweə(r)/

UNIT 5

accountant (n)   /ə'kaʊntənt/
ambition (n)   /æm'bɪʃn/
ambitious (adj)   /æm'bɪʃəs/
arrange (v) (= organize)   /ə'reɪndʒ/
arrival (n)   /ə'raɪvl/
attract (v)   /ə'trækt/
attraction (n)   /ə'trækʃn/
attractive (adj)   /ə'træktɪv/

bored (adj)   /bɔ:d/

chef (n)   /ʃef/
complain (v)   /kəm'pleɪn/
considerate (adj)   /kən'sɪdərət/
cook (v and n)   /kʊk/
cookbook (n)   /'kʊkbʊk/

decision (n)   /dɪ'sɪʒn/
degree (n)   /dɪ'gri:/

desperate (adj)   /'despərət/
documentary (n)   /dɒkjʊ'mentri/

134

earn (v) (money)   /ɜ:n/

fashion (n)   /'fæʃn/
fashionable (adj)   /'fæʃnəbl/
fed up (adj)   /fed 'ʌp/

get in touch (v) (= contact)   /get ɪn 'tʌtʃ/
get on with sb (v)   /get 'ɒn wɪð/
go out with sb (v)   /gəʊ 'aʊt wɪð/
go sightseeing (v)   /gəʊ 'saɪtsi:ɪŋ/

happiness (n)   /'hæpɪnəs/
health (n)   /helθ/

imagination (n)   /ɪmædʒɪ'neɪʃn/
imagine (v)   /ɪ'mædʒɪn/
improve (v)   /ɪm'pru:v/
improvement (n)   /ɪm'pru:vmənt/
invite (v)   /ɪn'vaɪt/

lazy (adj)   /'leɪzɪ/
lift (n) (= ride)   /lɪft/
lonely (adj)   /'ləʊnlɪ/

mansion (n)   /'mænʃn/
marketing (n)   /'mɑ:kətɪŋ/

notebook (n)   /'nəʊtbʊk/
nurse (n)   /nɜ:s/

own (v)   /əʊn/
own (adj)   /əʊn/

pick up (v) (= meet)   /pɪk 'ʌp/
politician (n)   /pɒlɪ'tɪʃn/
power (n)   /paʊə(r)/

sauce (n)   /sɔ:s/
science (n)   /'saɪəns/
scientific (adj)   /saɪən'tɪfɪk/
second-hand (adj)   /sekənd 'hænd/
share (v)   /ʃeə/
specialize (v)   /'speʃəlaɪz/
standard of living (n)   /stændəd əv 'lɪvɪŋ/
stick (v)   /stɪk/
succeed (v)   /sʌk'si:d/
success (n)   /sʌk'ses/
successful (adj)   /sʌk'sesfl/

tour company (n)   /'tʊə kʌmpənɪ/
train (v) (= learn, practise)   /treɪn/

well-paid (adj)   /wel' peɪd/

UNIT 6

across (prep)   /ə'krɒs/
along (prep)   /ə'lɒŋ/
annoyed (adj)   /ə'nɔɪd/
atmosphere (n) (of a place)   /'ætməsfɪə/
audience (n)   /'ɔ:dɪəns/
average (adj)   /'ævərɪdʒ/
awful (adj)   /'ɔ:fl/

break up (v) (a relationship)   /breɪk'ʌp/
bulb (n) (for light)   /bʌlb/

caring (adj)   /keərɪŋ/
cost (v)   /kɒst/
cost of living (n)   /kɒst əv 'lɪvɪŋ/
crowded (adj)   /'kraʊdɪd/

despite (prep)   /dɪ'spaɪt/

economical (adj)   /i:kə'nɒmɪkl/
exciting (adj)   /ɪk'saɪtɪŋ/
extravagant (adj)   /ɪk'strævəgənt/

fed up (adj)   /fed 'ʌp/
friendly (adj)   /'frendlɪ/

gate (n)   /geɪt/
generous (adj)   /'dʒenərəs/
get to know (v)   /get tə 'nəʊ/
guess (v)   /ges/

handsome (adj)   /'hænsəm/
hill (n)   /hɪl/

impatient (adj)   /ɪm'peɪʃnt/
impolite (adj)   /ɪmpə'laɪt/
impossible (adj)   /ɪm'pɒsəbl/
inconvenient (adj)   /ɪnkən'vi:nɪənt/
incorrect (adj)   /ɪnkə'rekt/
inexpensive (adj)   /ɪnɪk'spensɪv/

marvellous (adj)   /'mɑ:vələs/
mean (adj) (opp = generous)   /mi:n/
messy (adj)   /'mesɪ/
mixture (n)   /'mɪkstʃə/

naughty (adj)   /'nɔ:tɪ/
noisy (adj)   /'nɔɪzɪ/

orchestra (n)   /'ɔ:kɪstrə/
outgoing (adj) (person)   /aʊt'gəʊɪŋ/
over (prep)   /'əʊvə(r)/

palace (n)   /'pælɪs/
past (prep)   /pɑ:st/
path (n)   /pɑ:θ/
polluted (adj)   /pə'lu:tɪd/
pond (n)   /pɒnd/

quiet (adj)   /'kwaɪət/
quite (adj) (e.g. quite good)   /kwaɪt/

reserved (adj) (person)   /rɪ'zɜ:vd/

servant (n)   /'sɜ:vənt/
share (v)   /ʃeə(r)/
shy (adj)   /ʃaɪ/
snack (n)   /snæk/
spend (v) (money)   /spend/
staircase (n)   /'steəkeɪs/
suburb (n)   /'sʌbɜ:b/

temperature (n)   /'temprətʃə(r)/
through (prep)   /θru:/

ugly (adj)   /'ʌglɪ/
uncomfortable (adj)   /ʌn'kʌmftəbl/
unfriendly (adj)   /ʌn'frendlɪ/
unhappy (adj)   /ʌn'hæpɪ/
unimportant (adj)   /ʌnɪm'pɔ:tənt/
uninterested (adj)   /ʌn'ɪntrəstɪd/
untidy (adj)   /ʌn'taɪdɪ/

violinist (n)   /vaɪə'lɪnɪst/

wealth (n)   /welθ/
wealthy (adj)   /'welθɪ/

well-behaved (*adj*)   /wel bɪ'heɪvd/
wet (*adj*)   /wet/
whole (*adj*)   /həʊl/
wood (*n*) (= lots of trees)   /wʊd/

UNIT 7

abuse (*n*)   /ə'bju:s/
accident (*n*)   /'æksɪdənt/
act (*v*)   /ækt/
acting (*n*)   /'æktɪŋ/
actress (*n*)   /'æktrəs/
at last (*adv*)   /ət 'lɑ:st/
at least (*adv*)   /ət'li:st/
award (*n*)   /ə'wɔ:d/

brake (*n*)   /breɪk/
break (*v* and *n*)   /breɪk/

career (*n*)   /kə'rɪə(r)/
cause (*n*) (to fight for)   /kɔ:z/
charity (*n*)   /'tʃærətɪ/
check (*v*)   /tʃek/
cheque (*n*)   /tʃek/
childhood (*n*)   /'tʃaɪldhʊd/
concert (*n*)   /'kɒnsət/
conscience (*n*)   /'kɒnʃəns/
consider (*v*)   /kən'sɪdə(r)/

drum (*n*)   /drʌm/

environment (*n*)   /ɪn'vaɪrənmənt/
especially (*adv*)   /ɪ'speʃlɪ/
even (*adv*)   /'i:vn/
exactly (*adv*)   /ɪg'zæktlɪ/

fair (*adj*) (fair hair/decision)   /feə(r)/
fare (*n*)   /feə(r)/
fortunately (*adv*)   /'fɔ: tʃənətlɪ/

graduate (*v*)   /'grædʒʊeɪt/
guitar (*n*)   /gɪ'tɑ:(r)/

including (*prep*)   /ɪn'klu:dɪŋ/
influence (*v* and *n*)   /'ɪnflʊəns/
instrument (*n*) (musical)   /'ɪnstrʊmənt/
iron (*v*)   /'aɪən/

musician (*n*)   /mju:'zɪʃn/

nearly (*adv*)   /'nɪəlɪ/

of course (*adv*)   /əv'kɔ:s/
overdose (*n*)   /'əʊvədəʊs/

prize (*n*)   /praɪz/
prose (*n*)   /prəʊz/

race (*v* and *n*) (cars)   /reɪs/
recognize (*v*)   /'rekəgnaɪz/
record (*n*) (of music)   /'rekɔ:d/
rise (*n*) (to stardom)   /raɪz/
role (*n*)   /rəʊl/
roll (*v* nd *n*)   /rəʊl/

sail (*n*)   /seɪl/
sale (*n*)   /seɪl/
saxophone (*n*)   /'sæksəfəʊn/
several (*det*)   /'sevrəl/
shame (*n*)   /ʃeɪm/

slave (*n*)   /sleɪv/
stardom (*n*)   /'stɑ:dəm/
still (*adv*) (still in bed)   /stɪl/
support (*v* and *n*)   /sə'pɔ:t/

too (*adv*)   /tu:/
trumpet (*n*)   /'trʌmpɪt/

waist (*n*)   /weɪst/
waste (*v* and *n*)   /weɪst/
weak (*adj*)   /wi:k/
western (*n*)   /'westən/

UNIT 8

accept (*v*) (an invitation)   /ək'sept/
accommodation (*n*)   /əkɒmə'deɪʃn/
advantage (*n*)   /əd'vɑ:ntɪdʒ/
alarm clock (*n*)   /ə'lɑ:m klɒk/
argue (*v*)   /'ɑ:gju:/

bookcase (*n*)   /'bʊkkeɪs/
bully (*n*)   /'bʊlɪ/

cigarette lighter (*n*)   /sɪgə'ret laɪtə(r)/
consultant (*n*)   /kən'sʌltənt/
cool (*adj*) (weather)   /ku:l/
cruise (*n*)   /kru:z/
cry (*v*) (tears)   /kraɪ/

departure lounge (*n*)   /dɪ'pɑ:tʃə laʊndʒ/
disadvantage (*n*)   /dɪsəd'vɑ:ntɪdʒ/
document (*n*)   /'dɒkjʊmənt/
dustbin (*n*)   /'dʌstbɪn/
dye (*v* and *n*)   /daɪ/

ear-ring (*n*)   /'ɪərɪŋ/
earthquake (*n*)   /'ɜ:θkweɪk/
entertain (*v*)   /entə'teɪn/
equipment (*n*)   /ɪ'kwɪpmənt/
expert (*n*)   /'ekspɜ:t/

fame (*n*)   /feɪm/
favour (*n*)   /'feɪvə(r)/
fire engine (*n*)   /'faɪərendʒɪn/
fisherman (*n*)   /'fɪʃəmən/
fit (*adj*) (= healthy)   /fɪt/
furious (*adj*)   /'fjʊərɪəs/

hairdryer (*n*)   /'heədraɪə(r)/

impressed (*adj*)   /ɪm'prest/

lake (*n*)   /leɪk/
light (*adj*) (clothes)   /laɪt/

melt (*v*)   /melt/
mess (*n*)   /mes/
miner (*n*)   /maɪnə(r)/
model (*n*)   /'mɒdl/

notice-board (*n*)   /'nəʊtɪs bɔ:d/

original (*adj*)   /ə'rɪdʒənl/
overweight (*adj*)   /əʊvə'weɪt/

painful (*adj*)   /'peɪnfl/
pocket money (*n*)   /'pɒkɪt mʌnɪ/
pose (*v*)   /pəʊz/
program (*v* and *n*)
   (computers)   /'prəʊgræm/

project (n) /'prɒdʒekt/
punishment (n) /'pʌnɪʃmənt/

raincoat (n) /'reɪnkəʊt/
recommend (v) /rekə'mend/
refreshing (adj) /rɪ'freʃɪŋ/
refuse (v) (an invitation) /rɪ'fju:z/
remarkable (adj) /rɪ'mɑ:kəbl/
risk (n) /rɪsk/
rush hour (n) /'rʌʃ aʊə/

safety belt (n) /'seɪftɪ belt/
screwdriver (n) /'skru:draɪvə(r)/
shift (n) (work) /ʃɪft/
signpost (n) /'saɪnpəʊst/
speciality (n) /speʃɪ'ælətɪ/
speech (n) /spi:tʃ/
software (n) (computers) /'sɒftweə/
stamina (n) /'stæmɪnə/
standard (n) /'stændəd/
sunset (n) /'sʌnset/
swimming costume (n) /'swɪmɪŋ kɒstju:m/

tape-recorder (n) /'teɪp rɪkɔ:də(r)/
tasty (adj) /'teɪstɪ/
tease (v) /ti:z/
timetable (n) /'taɪmteɪbl/
tin-opener (n) /'tɪn əʊpənə/
toothpaste (n) /'tu:θpeɪst/
traffic lights (n) /'træfɪk laɪts/

uniform (n) /'ju:nɪfɔ:m/

valuable (adj) /'væljʊəbl/
variety (n) /və'raɪətɪ/
vegetarian (n) /vedʒɪ'teərɪən/
vet (n) /vet/

watch repairer (n) /'wɒtʃ rɪpeərə(r)/
waterproof (adj) /'wɔ:təpru:f/
word processor (n) /'wɜ:d prəʊsesə(r)/
worth (adj) /wɜ:θ/

UNIT 9

according to (prep) /ə'kɔ:dɪŋ tʊ/
architect (n) /'ɑ:kitekt/
area (n) /'eərɪə/
aware of (adj) /ə'weə(r) əv/

board (v) (a plane, boat) /bɔ:d/
boarding card (n) /'bɔ:dɪŋ kɑ:d/
buffet car (n) /'bʊfeɪ kɑ:(r)/

case (n) (suitcase) /keɪs/
catch (v) (a train) /kætʃ/
cause (n) (= reason) /kɔ:z/
characteristic (n) /kærəktə'rɪstɪk/
check in (v) /tʃek 'ɪn/
check-in desk (n) /'tʃek ɪn desk/
choice (n) /tʃɔɪs/
compartment (n) (in a train) /kəm'pɑ:tmənt/
contain (v) /kən'teɪn/

double (v) /'dʌbl/
duty-free shop (n) /dju:tɪ 'fri: ʃɒp/

either (det) /aɪðə(r)/
environmentalist (n) /ɪnvaɪrən'mentəlɪst/

gate (n) (at an airport) /geɪt/

height (n) /haɪt/
huge (adj) /hju:dʒ/

injure (v) /'ɪndʒə/
invention (n) /ɪn'venʃn/

jam (n) (traffic) /dʒæm/

less (det) /les/
lift (n) /lɪft/
look after (v) /lʊk 'ɑ:ftə(r)/
luggage (n) /'lʌgɪdʒ/

miss (v) (a train/plane) /mɪs/

need (n) /ni:d/

passenger (n) /'pæsɪndʒə(r)/
platform (n) /'plætfɔ:m/
protect (v) /prə'tekt/

race (n) (of people) /reɪs/
recycle (v) /ri:'saɪkl/
research (v and n) /rɪ'sɜ:tʃ/
return (n) (ticket) /rɪ'tɜ:n/
robot (n) /'rəʊbɒt/

shorts (n) /ʃɔ:ts/
single (ticket) (n) /'sɪŋgl/
survey (n) /'sɜ:veɪ/
survive (v) /sə'vaɪv/
symbol (n) /'sɪmbl/

ticket inspector (n) /'tɪkɪt ɪnspektə(r)/
ticket office (n) /'tɪkɪt ɒfɪs/
traffic jam (n) /'træfɪk dʒæm/
trolley (n) /'trɒlɪ/

unfasten (v) /ʌn'fɑ:sn/
unleaded petrol (n) /'ʌnledɪd' petrəl/

waiting room (n) /'weɪtɪŋ ru:m/

UNIT 10

argument (n) /'ɑ:gjʊmənt/
athlete (n) /'æθli:t/

ban (v) /bæn/
belong (v) /bɪ'lɒŋ/
bikini (n) /bɪ'ki:nɪ/
blouse (n) /blaʊz/
break the law (v) /breɪk ðə 'lɔ:/
bull (n) /bʊl/

cause (n) (to fight) /kɔ:z/
chain (v and n) /tʃeɪn/
cleaner (n) /'kli:nə(r)/
countryside (n) /'kʌntrɪsaɪd/
courageous (adj) /kə'reɪdʒəs/
cousin (n) /'kʌzn/
crowd (n) /kraʊd/

demand (v) /dɪ'mɑ:nd/
dream (v and n) /dri:m/
duchess (n) /'dʌtʃɪs/

duke (n)   /dju:k/
emotional (adj)   /ɪˈməʊʃənl/
encourage (v)   /ɪnˈkʌrɪdʒ/
event (n)   /ɪˈvent/

fight (v and n)   /faɪt/

hero (n)   /ˈhɪərəʊ/
heroine (n)   /ˈherəʊɪn/

judge (n)   /dʒʌdʒ/

landlady (n)   /ˈlændleɪdɪ/
landlord (n)   /ˈlændlɔːd/
law (n)   /lɔː/
legal (adj)   /ˈliːgl/

mainly (adv)   /ˈmeɪnlɪ/
march (v and n)   /mɑːtʃ/
martyr (n)   /ˈmɑːtə(r)/
memory (n)   /ˈmemərɪ/
mini-skirt (n)   /ˈmɪnɪskɜːt/
movement (n) (political)   /ˈmuːvmənt/

nephew (n)   /ˈnefjuː/
niece (n)   /niːs/
notice (v)   /ˈneʊtɪs/

opposition (n)   /ɒpəˈzɪʃn/
organize (v)   /ˈɔːgənaɪz/

peaceful (adj)   /ˈpiːsfl/
petition (n)   /pəˈtɪʃn/
pie (n)   /paɪ/
pop concert (n)   /ˈpɒp kɒnsət/
professor (n)   /prəˈfesə(r)/
publicity (n)   /pʌbˈlɪsətɪ/
pyjamas (n)   /pəˈdʒɑːməz/

reasonable (adj) (= not expensive)   /ˈriːznəbl/
refuse (v)   /rɪˈfjuːz/
right (n) (to do something)   /raɪt/

scientist (n)   /ˈsaɪəntɪst/
shock (v)   /ʃɒk/
shocking (adj)   /ˈʃɒkɪŋ/
sociable (adj)   /ˈsəʊʃəbl/
spoil (v) (a child)   /spɔɪl/
surprised (adj)   /səˈpraɪzd/

teenager (n)   /ˈtiːneɪdʒə(r)/

underpants (n)   /ˈʌndəpænts/

vote (v and n)   /vəʊt/

widow (n)   /ˈwɪdəʊ/
widower (n)   /ˈwɪdəʊə/

UNIT 11

anniversary (n)   /ænɪˈvɜːsərɪ/
apologize (v)   /əˈpɒlədʒaɪz/

bargain (n)   /ˈbɑːgɪn/
beetle (n)   /ˈbiːtl/
belong (v)   /bɪˈlɒŋ/

celebrate (v)   /ˈselɪbreɪt/
(in) charge (n)   /tʃɑːdʒ/
chat (v and n)   /tʃæt/

competition (n)   /kɒmpəˈtɪʃn/
consumer (n)   /kənˈsjuːmə(r)/

depend (v)   /dɪˈpend/
deserve (v)   /dɪˈzɜːv/
design (v and n)   /dɪˈzaɪn/
disease (n)   /dɪˈziːz/
distinctive (adj)   /dɪˈstɪŋktɪv/
due to (prep)   /ˈdjuː tʊ/

ear-rings (n)   /ˈɪərɪŋz/
energy (n)   /ˈenədʒɪ/

factory (n)   /ˈfæktərɪ/
fan (n) (person)   /fæn/
furious (adj)   /ˈfjʊərɪəs/

generosity (n)   /dʒenəˈrɒsɪtɪ/
graceful (adj)   /ˈgreɪsfl/
grow (v) (e.g. rice)   /grəʊ/

heart (n)   /hɑːt/
honesty (n)   /ˈɒnəstɪ/

invent (v)   /ɪnˈvent/
invention (n)   /ɪnˈvenʃən/

lottery (n)   /ˈlɒtərɪ/

manufacture (v)   /mænjʊˈfæktʃə(r)/

operate (v)   /ˈɒpəreɪt/
owner (n)   /ˈəʊnə(r)/

parachute (n)   /ˈpærəʃuːt/
pot of tea (n)   /pɒt əv ˈtiː/
produce (v)   /prəˈdjuːs/

raise (v) (money)   /reɪz/
refreshment (n)   /rɪˈfreʃmənt/
reliable (adj)   /rɪˈlaɪəbl/
reward (n)   /rɪˈwɔːd/
rope (n)   /rəʊp/

settle (v) (in a place)   /ˈsetl/
spare (adj)   /speə(r)/
speed (n)   /spiːd/
stable (n) (for horses)   /ˈsteɪbl/
stocking (n)   /ˈstɒkɪŋ/
suffer (v)   /ˈsʌfə(r)/

tidy (v)   /ˈtaɪdɪ/
transplant (n)   /ˈtrænsplɑːnt/

upset (adj)   /ʌpˈset/

wave (v) (your hand)   /weɪv/
will (n) (= testament)   /wɪl/

UNIT 12

adventure (n)   /ədˈventʃə(r)/
authority (n)   /ɔːˈθɒrɪtɪ/

battle (n)   /ˈbætl/
behave (v)   /bɪˈheɪv/
bleed (v)   /bliːd/
bored (adj)   /bɔːd/
boring (adj)   /ˈbɔːrɪŋ/
bow and arrow (n)   /bəʊ ənd ˈærəʊ/
brave (adj)   /breɪv/
bury (v)   /ˈberɪ/

capture (*v*) /ˈkæptʃə(r)/
carefully (*adv*) /ˈkeəfəlɪ/
castle (*n*) /ˈkɑːsl/
chase (*v*) /tʃeɪs/
clearly (*adv*) /ˈklɪəlɪ/
creep (*v*) /kriːp/

deer (*n*) /dɪə(r)/
defeat (*v*) /dɪˈfiːt/
defend (*v*) /dɪˈfend/
dragon (*n*) /ˈdrægən/

embarrassed (*adj*) /ɪmˈbærəst/
embarrassing (*adj*) /ɪmˈbærəsɪŋ/
emperor (*n*) /ˈempərə(r)/
enemy (*n*) /ˈenəmɪ/
equal (*adj*) /ˈiːkwəl/
escape (*v*) /ɪˈskeɪp/
extraordinary (*adj*) /ɪkˈstrɔːdnrɪ/

flash of lightning (*n*) /flæʃ əv ˈlaɪtnɪŋ/
fluently (*adv*) /ˈfluːəntlɪ/
forest (*n*) /ˈfɒrɪst/
forever (*adv*) /fəˈrevə(r)/
frightened (*adj*) /ˈfraɪtənd/

giant (*n*) /ˈdʒaɪənt/
grab (*v*) /græb/
guide (*v and n*) /gaɪd/

heat (*n*) /hiːt/
honour (*n*) /ˈɒnə(r)/
hunt (*v and n*) /hʌnt/

injustice (*n*) /ɪnˈdʒʌstɪs/
interested (*adj*) /ˈɪntrəstɪd/
interesting (*adj*) /ˈɪntrəstɪŋ/
invasion (*n*) /ɪnˈveɪʒn/

kingdom (*n*) /ˈkɪŋdəm/

leader (*n*) /ˈliːdə(r)/
legend (*n*) /ˈledʒənd/
let (sb do) (*v*) /let/

magician (*n*) /məˈdʒɪʃn/
make (sb do) (*v*) /meɪk/
manage (to do) (*v*) /ˈmænɪdʒ/

off-licence (*n*) /ˈɒf laɪsəns/

poison (*v and n*) /ˈpɔɪzn/
properly (*adv*) /ˈprɒpəlɪ/
protect (*v*) /prəˈtekt/
prove (*v*) /pruːv/

receive (*v*) /rɪˈsiːv/
respect (*n*) /rɪˈspekt/
rob (*v*) /rɒb/
robber (*n*) /ˈrɒbə(r)/

self-defence (*n*) /self dɪˈfens/
snake (*n*) /sneɪk/
suddenly (*adv*) /ˈsʌdənlɪ/
surprised (*adj*) /səˈpraɪzd/
surprising (*adj*) /səˈpraɪzɪŋ/
sword (*n*) /sɔːd/

tell (sb to do) (*v*) /tel/
tired (*adj*) /taɪəd/
tiring (*adj*) /ˈtaɪərɪŋ/
throat (*n*) /θrəʊt/

view (*n*) /vjuː/

wild (*adj*) /waɪəld/
wounded (*adj*) /ˈwuːndɪd/

UNIT 13

amazing (*adj*) /əˈmeɪzɪŋ/
analyse (*v*) /ˈænəlaɪz/

behaviour (*n*) /bɪˈheɪvjə(r)/
belief (*n*) /bɪˈliːf/
block of flats (*n*) /blɒk əv ˈflæts/
bring up (*v*) (children) /brɪŋ ˈʌp/
budgie (*n*) /ˈbʌdʒɪ/
burglar (*n*) /ˈbɜːglə(r)/

chauffeur (*n*) /ˈʃəʊfə(r)/
confident (*adj*) /ˈkɒnfɪdənt/
contents (*n*) /ˈkɒntents/
cosmopolitan (*adj*) /kɒzməˈpɒlɪtən/
costume (*n*) /ˈkɒstjuːm/
cottage (*n*) /ˈkɒtɪdʒ/
crown (*n*) /kraʊn/

death (*n*) /deθ/

edge (*n*) /edʒ/
experience (*n*) /ɪkˈspɪərɪəns/

fail (*v*) (an exam) /feɪl/
fantasy (*n*) /ˈfæntəsɪ/
fear (*v and n*) /fɪə/

get on with (*v*) /get ˈɒn wɪð/
goldfish (*n*) /ˈgəʊldfɪʃ/
governess (*n*) /ˈgʌvənɪs/

hurry up (*v*) /hʌrɪ ˈʌp/

image (*n*) /ˈɪmɪdʒ/
interpretation (*n*) /ɪntɜːprɪˈteɪʃn/

lack (*n*) /læk/
lie down (*v*) /laɪ ˈdaʊn/
look for (*v*) /ˈlʊk fɔː/
look forward to (*v*) /lʊk ˈfɔːwəd tʊ/
look up (*v*) (in a dictionary) /lʊk ˈʌp/

management (*n*) /ˈmænɪdʒmənt/
memorable (*adj*) /ˈmemərəbl/
mix (*n*) /mɪks/
mixed (*adj*) /mɪkst/

narrow (*adj*) /ˈnærəʊ/
nervous (*adj*) /ˈnɜːvəs/

optimistic (*adj*) /ɒptɪˈmɪstɪk/

pass (*v*) (an exam) /pɑːs/
peacock (*n*) /ˈpiːkɒk/
personality (*n*) /pɜːsəˈnælətɪ/
pessimistic (*adj*) /pesɪˈmɪstɪk/
pool (*n*) /puːl/
positive (*adj*) /ˈpɒzɪtɪv/
prepare (*v*) /prɪˈpeə(r)/
put on (*v*) (clothes) /pʊtˈɒn/
put out (*v*) (a cigarette) /pʊtˈaʊt/

relative (*n*) (family) /ˈrelətɪv/
religion (*n*) /rɪˈlɪdʒən/
romantic (*adj*) /rəʊˈmæntɪk/
ruin (*v and n*) /ˈruːɪn/

shape (n)   /ʃeɪp/
stand up (v)   /stænd 'ʌp/
sweater (n)   /'swetə(r)/
switch off (v) (a light)   /swɪtʃ 'ɒf/

take off (v) (clothes)   /teɪk 'ɒf/
take off (v) (a plane)   /teɪk 'ɒf/
throw away (v)   /θrəʊ ə'weɪ/
track suit (n)   /'træk suːt/
traditional (adj)   /trə'dɪʃənl/
turn down (v) (a radio)   /tɜːn 'daʊn/
turn off (v) (a light)   /tɜːn 'ɒf/

valuable (adj)   /'væljʊəbl/

wave (n) (in the sea)   /weɪv/
weather forecast (n)   /'weðə fɔːkɑːst/
wedding (n)   /'wedɪŋ/

UNIT 14

accommodate (v)   /ə'kɒmədeɪt/
active (adj)   /'æktɪv/
advertise (v)   /'ædvətaɪz/
approach (v)   /ə'prəʊtʃ/
archeology (n)   /ɑːkɪ'ɒlədʒɪ/
argument (n)   /'ɑːgjʊmənt/
arrival (n)   /ə'raɪvl/

burn (v and n)   /bɜːn/

careless (adj)   /'keələs/
celebration (n)   /selɪ'breɪʃn/
comfort (n)   /'kʌmfət/
commute (v)   /kə'mjuːt/
computerize (v)   /kəm'pjuːtəraɪz/
crew (n)   /kruː/
crime (n)   /kraɪm/

daily (adj)   /'deɪlɪ/
departure (n)   /dɪ'pɑːtʃə(r)/
deserted (adj)   /dɪ'zɜːtɪd/
determination (n)   /dɪtɜːmɪ'neɪʃn/
development (n)   /dɪ'veləpmənt/
disappear (v)   /dɪsə'pɪə(r)/
discovery (n)   /dɪ'skʌvərɪ/
discuss (v)   /dɪ'skʌs/
dishonest (adj)   /dɪs'ɒnɪst/
drown (v)   /draʊn/

existence (n)   /ɪg'zɪstəns/

favour (n)   /'feɪvə(r)/
flight (n)   /flaɪt/

generosity (n)   /dʒenə'rɒsɪtɪ/
get engaged (v)   /get ɪn'geɪdʒd/
govern (v)   /'gʌvən/
growth (n)   /grəʊθ/

hire (v)   /haɪə(r)/
honeymoon (n)   /'hʌnɪmuːn/
hopefully (adv)   /'həʊpfʊlɪ/

invent (v)   /ɪn'vent/

jam (v and n)   /dʒæm/

leather (n)   /'leðə(r)/
lipstick (n)   /'lɪpstɪk/

lose weight (v)   /luːz 'weɪt/

message (n)   /'mesɪdʒ/
mist (n)   /mɪst/

operate (v)   /'ɒpəreɪt/
order (v) (a meal)   /ɔːdə(r)/

reception (n) (wedding)   /rɪ'sepʃn/
reliability (n)   /rɪlaɪə'bɪlətɪ/
route (n)   /ruːt/

stopover (n)   /'stɒpəʊvə(r)/

takeaway (n)   /'teɪkəweɪ/
technology (n)   /tek'nɒlədʒɪ/
term (n) (school)   /tɜːm/

useless (adj)   /'juːsləs/

value (v)   /'væljuː/

wake up (v)   /weɪk 'ʌp/
wellington boot (n)   /welɪŋtən 'buːt/

UNIT 15

alone (adj)   /ə'ləʊn/

barn (n)   /bɑːn/
bring (v)   /brɪŋ/

desperate (adj)   /'despərət/
detective story (n)   /dɪ'tektɪv stɔːrɪ/
downpour (n)   /'daʊnpɔː(r)/

except (prep)   /ɪk'sept/

fall in love (v)   /'fɔːl ɪn 'lʌv/
football pools (n)   /'fʊtbɔːl puːlz/
forever (adv)   /fə'revə(r)/

get better (v)   /get 'betə(r)/
get cold (v)   /get 'kəʊld/
get ready (v)   /get 'redɪ/

immoral (adj)   /ɪ'mɒrəl/

last (v)   /lɑːst/

moral (n)   /'mɒrəl/

pack (v)   /pæk/
parable (n)   /'pærəbl/
passionately (adv)   /'pæʃənətlɪ/
power (n)   /paʊə(r)/
pretend (v)   /prɪ'tend/

react (v)   /rɪ'ækt/
regret (v)   /rɪ'gret/
regularly (adv)   /'regjʊləlɪ/
resist (v)   /rɪ'zɪst/
rubbish bin (n)   /'rʌbɪʃ bɪn/

seek (v)   /siːk/
shelter (v and n)   /'ʃeltə(r)/
suspect (v)   /sʌ'spekt/
suspicious (adj)   /sə'spɪʃəs/

temptation (n)   /temp'teɪʃn/

Appendix 1

Irregular verbs

Base form	Past Simple	Past Participle
be	was/were	been
become	became	become
begin	began	begun
blow	blew	blown
break	broke	broken
bring	brought	brought
build	built	built
burn	burnt	burnt
buy	bought	bought
can	could	been able
catch	caught	caught
choose	chose	chosen
come	came	come
cost	cost	cost
cut	cut	cut
do	did	done
draw	drew	drawn
dream	dreamt	dreamt
drink	drank	drunk
drive	drove	driven
eat	ate	eaten
fall	fell	fallen
feel	felt	felt
find	found	found
fly	flew	flown
forget	forgot	forgotten
get	got	got
give	gave	given
go	went	gone
grow	grew	grown
have	had	had
hear	heard	heard
hit	hit	hit
hold	held	held
hurt	hurt	hurt
keep	kept	kept
know	knew	known
lead	led	led
learn	learnt	learnt
leave	left	left
lend	lent	lent
lose	lost	lost
make	made	made
mean	meant	meant
meet	met	met
must	had to	had to
pay	paid	paid
put	put	put
read	read	read
ring	rang	rung
rise	rose	risen
run	ran	run
say	said	said
see	saw	seen
sell	sold	sold
send	sent	sent
show	showed	shown
shut	shut	shut

Base form	Past Simple	Past Participle
sing	sang	sung
sink	sank	sunk
sit	sat	sat
sleep	slept	slept
speak	spoke	spoken
spend	spent	spent
stand	stood	stood
steal	stole	stolen
swim	swam	swum
take	took	taken
teach	taught	taught
tear	tore	torn
tell	told	told
think	thought	thought
throw	threw	thrown
understand	understood	understood
wake	woke	woken
wear	wore	worn
win	won	won
write	wrote	written

Appendix 2

Word + preposition

(sb = somebody   sth = something)

(break sth) by accident
according to (the weather forecast)
an advertisement for sth
afraid of (dogs)
at the age of (six)
(I don't) agree with (you).
(to) apply for (a job)
(to) argue with sb about sth
(to) arrive at (the station) = at a place
(to) arrive in (England) = in a country
(to) ask for sth
(to be) aware of (a problem)

(to) believe in (God)
(to) belong to sb
(to be) bored with sb/sth
(go) by bus, train, car

in the (19th) century
(Have you got) change for (a pound)?
(I'm) in charge.
on the coast
(I) come from (Scotland).
Compared with (other schools, this one is
     cheap).
(to) complain about (the food)
in (good) condition

(to) deal with (a problem)
(She has a) degree in (English literature).
(to) depend on (the weather)
(to) develop into (a big business)
(to) die of (a heart attack)
(to be) different from/to sb/sth
(Your country is) different from/to (mine).
in the distance
(to) dream about sb/sth

(to be) fed up with sb/sth
(to) fight against sb/sth
(to) find out about sb/sth
on a flight to (London)
(to live) on the (third) floor
(to) forget about sb/sth
(to be) full of (energy)

(to) get on (well) with sb
(to) go out with sb = be boyfriend and
     girlfriend
(to be) good at sth

(to be) on holiday
(to be) at home (But (to) go home)

(to be) impressed by sb/sth
(to be) interested in sb/sth
(to have) an interview for a job
(to) invite sb to (a party) or for (dinner)

(to) laugh at sb/sth
(to) listen to sb/sth

(to) look after (sb who is ill)
(to) look at (a picture)
(to) look for (sth you have lost)
(to) look forward to (a holiday)
(to be) in love with sb
(We've got lamb) for (lunch/dinner).

(to be) married to sb
(The room's) in a mess.

in the north/south

(to) operate on sb
(This machine's) out of order.

(to) pay (£500) for (a car)
(to) point (a gun) at sb/sth

(to) rely on sb/sth
as a result

(to) sell sth for (£300)
(to) share sth with sb
(Your shirt is) similar to (mine).
(to) speak to sb about sth
(to) spend money on (clothes)
(to) steal sth from sb
a story about sb/sth
(to be) on strike for (more money)
(to) suffer from sth

(to) talk to sb about sth
     on television
(to) think about (What are you thinking
     about?)
(to) think of (What do you think of Van
     Gogh?)
(to) throw (tomatoes) at sb
a ticket for (a concert)
(to be) tired of sb/sth
(to get) in touch with sb

(to) wait for sb/sth
on the way (to school)
(to) work as (a teacher)
(to) work for (an organization)
(to) worry about sb/sth
to write (a letter) to sb

Prepositions of time

in
in the morning/afternoon/evening
     January, etc.
     summer, etc.
     1985
     the 1920s
     two weeks
     two weeks' time
     your free time

at
at six o'clock, etc.
     midnight
     Christmas/Easter
     the weekend
     the moment

on
on Saturday, etc.
     Monday morning, etc.
     18 January, etc.

for
for six minutes, etc.
     a long time
     ages

since
since 18 July, etc.
     my last birthday
     I arrived

during
during the film/lesson/war/holidays/winter
(Notice that **while** is used **with** a subject
and a verb:
While I was on holiday
               watching the film
               coming to school . . .)

Appendix 3

Verb patterns

Verb + *-ing*	
like love enjoy finish	swimming cooking

Verb + *to* + infinitive	
agree choose decide expect forget help hope manage promise refuse try want would like would love would prefer	to go to work

Note

Help can be used without **to**:
He helped do the shopping.

Have for obligation is followed by **to + infinitive**.
I have to go now. Goodbye.

Notice the expression **take** + a time + **to** + infinitive
It takes twenty minutes to get here.

Used to for past habits is followed by the infinitive.
People used to think the earth was flat.

Verb + *ing* or *to* + infinitive	
begin continue start	raining/to rain working/to work

Verb + sb + *to* + infinitive		
advise ask encourage expect help invite tell want	some- body	to go to study to come

Verb + sb + infinitive (no *to*)		
let make	somebody	go do

Modal auxiliary verbs	
can could shall should might must will would	go arrive

Acknowledgements

The authors would like to thank Tim Lowe and Jeremy Page for their invaluable comments on the manuscript; and all the staff at Oxford University Press.

The publishers and authors are grateful to the following teachers and institutions for piloting sample units and for providing invaluable comment and feedback on the manuscript:

Dawn Dogna
Florence Durand
Sarah Ellis
Richard Felski
Jane Glover
Bridget Green
Claire Grob
James Hunter
Mark Rignall

A.V.L.
The British Institute, Barcelona
The British Institute, Florence
International House, London
International House, Barcelona
International House, Mataró

The publishers would like to thank students at International House, London, for providing the script for 'Hello' in Arabic, Italian, Japanese, and Spanish.

The publishers and authors would like to thank the following for their kind permission to use extracts and adaptations from copyright material:
Carlin Music Corporation: lyrics from *The Girl of my Best Friend* by Beverley Ross and Sam Bobrick; p. 117.
Coca-Cola Great Britain: extract from 'Things go better with Coca-Cola'; p. 77.
Exley Publications and Dominic Poelsma for two cartoons from *Beware of the Teenager* by Pam Brown; p. 62.
Garth Publications: extract from 'Call David – he's digital dynamite' in *Early Times*, the newspaper for young people. (Photo posed by model.) 19 January 1989; p. 60.
Glidrose Publications: extract from *The Man with the Golden Gun* by Ian Fleming; p. 22.
The *Independent*: extract from 'Living in the skies' by Louise Hidalgo, 1 February 1990; p. 65.
Oxford University Press: dictionary entries from *Oxford Elementary Learner's Dictionary of English*, p. 24; *Oxford French Minidictionary*; p. 10.
Pan Books: extract from *Airport International* by Brian Moynahan; p. 81.
Today: extract from 'Desperately seeking someone' by Margaret Morrison, 5 October 1989; p. 38.

The publishers and authors thank the following for permission to use recorded material from radio commercials:

Coca-Cola Great Britain, Dewynters plc, Motorfair, P&O European Ferries, Ross

The publishers have been unable to trace the copyright holders of *Sing a Song of Motor Cars*.

The publishers would like to thank the following for their permission to reproduce photographs:
Aquarius Picture Library p. 52 (film still), p. 82 ('Herbie')
A V Distributors (London) Ltd/Chris Allan Aviation Library pp. 106/107 (BA Plane)
Art Directors Photo Library pp. 106/107 (sky background)
Barnabys Picture Library p. 12, p. 18, p. 32 Bill Meadows (Post Office), (Harrods), p. 34 (children), p. 55 Paul Seaman (surfing)
Camera Press p. 24, p. 72 (Berlin Wall, Beatles)
Coca-Cola UK p. 77
Suki Coe p. 76 ('Camilla')
Collections/Roy Stedall-Humphryes p. 7 (castle)
Bruce Coleman Ltd p. 84 (snarling tiger)
James David Photography p. 14 (Edinburgh), p. 34 (Maldives), p. 41, p. 42 (London and Rome), p. 63 (skiers, Lake Brienz, seafood, Egypt/ mosque at sunset)
Greg Evans Photo Library p. 19
Mary Evans Picture Library p. 88
Express Newspapers/Barry Lewis p. 61 (Kimora/ schoolgirl)
Robert Harding Picture Library p. 42 (New York), Nigel Blythe (Tokyo), p. 46 Walter Rawlings (London pub, Madrid café), p. 55 (hot air balloon), p. 63 (fondue, Swiss restaurant, Ipanema beach, Cairo/mosque), p. 69 GR Richardson, p. 79 (parachute), p. 80 (concorde, Tudor house)
Heathrow Airport Picture Library pp. 106/107 (all black and white apart from aerial view)
Hulton Picture Company p. 71 (Charleston, Chaplin), p. 72 (1960s dress, Ban the Bomb), p. 74, p. 75
Katz Eyes p. 23
Annie Loire p. 95 ('Mike')
Marks and Spencer p. 29
National Motor Museum Picture Library/Beaulieu p. 82 (Beetle)
Quadrant Picture Library pp. 106,107 (Heathrow: entrance, aerial view, Aerodrome 1930)
Rex Features p. 44, p. 61/Barthelemy (catwalk portrait)
John and Liz Soars p. 46 (Kate Leigh) p. 54, p. 55, p. 71 (girl in car), p. 76 ('Bill Cole')
Frank Spooner/Gamma p. 52 (Paul Newman/racing gear and with Joanne Woodward)
Stoddard Carpets Ltd p. 76 (carpet manufacture)
Syndication International (Britain on View) p. 32 (bakery/Paddington Station), p. 55 (walking)
Syndication International p. 79 (two models)
John Walmsley p. 93

Illustrations by:
Mike Allport pp. 35, 85, 96, 97, 108, 109, 110, 111
Julie Anderson pp. 6, 17, 57, 100, 102, 103, 112, 113, 118
Kevin Baverstock p. 41
Jenny Brackley pp. 9, 116, 117
Phil Gascoine p. 22
Robina Green pp. 19, 92, 115

Roland Harmer p. 47
Nick Harris pp. 28, 101, 102
Vanessa Luff pp. 27, 30, 31
Bob Moulder p. 87
David Murray pp. 22, 89, 91, 92, 114
Nigel Paige pp. 2, 50, 66, 78, 90, 98
Nick Sharratt pp. 36, 37, 105
Raymond Turvey pp. 13, 16, 17, 18, 45, 65
David Williams p. 68
Willow p. 73

Location photography by:
Rob Judges (portraits) pp. 7, 40, 48, 49, 67, 86
Ander McIntyre (portraits) pp. 7, 11, 14, 16, 33, 38, 56, 58, 60, 63, 80, 99, 113

Studio photography by:
Garry and Marilyn O'Brien pp. 10, 25, 26, 32, 52

Every effort has been made to trace the owners of copyright material used in this book, but we should be pleased to hear from any copyright holder whom we have been unable to contact.

Oxford University Press
Walton Street, Oxford OX2 6DP

Oxford   New York
Athens   Auckland   Bangkok   Bombay
Calcutta   Cape Town   Dar es Salaam   Delhi
Florence   Hong Kong   Istanbul   Karachi
Kuala Lumpur   Madras   Madrid   Melbourne
Mexico City   Nairobi   Paris   Singapore
Taipei   Tokyo   Toronto

and associated companies in Berlin   Ibadan

OXFORD and OXFORD ENGLISH are trade marks of Oxford University Press

ISBN 0 19 433987 4   International Edition

© Oxford University Press 1991

First published 1991
Seventeenth impression 1996

Phototypeset in 10.5/12pt Times by Tradespools Limited, Frome, Somerset, England

Printed in Hong Kong